THE DEMAND
FOR PHYSICAL CAPITAL:
APPLICATION
OF A WEALTH MODEL

THE DEMAND

FOR PHYSICAL CAPITAL:

APPLICATION

OF A WEALTH MODEL

FREDERICK S. HAMMER

Assistant Vice President
Bankers Trust Company

PRENTICE-HALL, INC.
Englewood Cliffs, N. J.

L.C. Catalog Card Number 64–17014

· *Printed in the United States of America*
19796C

1960 Award Winners

Bernard H. Baum *Decentralization of Authority in a Bureaucracy*
Dissertation submitted to Department of Sociology, University of Chicago

Leon V. Hirsch *Marketing in an Underdeveloped Economy: The North Indian Sugar Industry*
Dissertation submitted to Graduate School of Business Administration, Harvard University

Bedros Peter Pashigian *The Distribution of Automobiles, an Economic Analysis of the Franchise System*
Dissertation submitted to Department of Economics, Massachusetts Institute of Technology

Martin Patchen *The Choice of Wage Comparison*
Dissertation submitted to Department of Social Psychology, University of Michigan

Fred M. Tonge *A Heuristic Program for Assembly Line Balancing*
Dissertation submitted to Graduate School of Industrial Administration, Carnegie Institute of Technology

1959 Award Winners

Kalman J. Cohen *Computer Models of the Shoe, Leather, Hide Sequence*
Dissertation submitted to Graduate School of Industrial Administration, Carnegie Institute of Technology

Bob R. Holdren *The Structure of a Retail Market and the Market Behavior of Retail Units*
Dissertation submitted to Department of Economics, Yale University

Frank Proschan *Polya Type Distributions in Renewal Theory, with an Application to an Inventory Problem*
Dissertation submitted to Department of Statistics, Stanford University

Andrew C. Stedry *Budget Control and Cost Behavior*
Dissertation submitted to Graduate School of Industrial Administration, Carnegie Institute of Technology

Victor H. Vroom *Some Personality Determinants of the Effects of Participation*
Dissertation submitted to Department of Psychology, University of Michigan

1962 Award Winners

Alexander Barges *The Effect of Capital Structure on the Cost of Capital*
Dissertation submitted to Graduate School of Business Administration, Northwestern University

Chalres P. Bonini *Simulation of Information and Decision Systems in the Firm*
Dissertation submitted to Graduate School of Business, Carnegie Institute of Technology

James M. Ferguson *The Advertising Rate Structure in the Daily Newspaper Industry*
Dissertation submitted to Department of Economics, University of Chicago

Gordon M. Kaufman *Statistical Decision and Related Techniques in Oil and Gas Exploration*
Dissertation submitted to Graduate School of Business, Harvard University

H. Martin Weingartner *Mathematical Programming and the Analysis of Capital Budgeting Problems*
Dissertation submitted to Graduate School of Industrial Administration Carnegie Institute of Technology

1961 Award Winners

Geoffrey P. E. Clarkson *Portfolio Selection: A Simulation of Trust Investment*
Dissertation submitted to Graduate School of Industrial Administration, Carnegie Institute of Technology

Donald E. Farrar *The Investment Decision Under Uncertainty: Portfolio Selection*
Dissertation submitted to Faculty of Arts and Sciences, Harvard University

Richard S. Hatch *An Evaluation of a Forced-Choice Differential Accuracy Approach to the Measurement of Supervisory Empathy*
Dissertation submitted to Department of Psychology, University of Minnesota

David Meiselman *The Term Structure of Interest Rates*
Dissertation submitted to Department of Economics, University of Chicago

George William Summers *Financing and Initial Operations of New Firms*
Dissertation submitted to Department of Management, Case Institute of Technology

Foreword

Dr. Hammer's dissertation, completed during the academic year 1962–1963, is one of six selected for publication in the fifth annual Doctoral Dissertation Competition sponsored by the Program in Economic Development and Administration of the Ford Foundation.

The intent of the doctoral dissertation competition has been to recognize and encourage excellence in research on business by graduate students. Publication awards, now totaling twenty-six, have been made over the five years of the competition to persons granted doctorates in business and related fields whose thesis research on problems of business was especially distinguished by its analytical content and strong roots in the underlying disciplines common to business.

In addition to Dr. Hammer's, the dissertations published this year are:

The Demand for Liquid Assets: A Temporal Cross-Section Analysis
  Edgar Louis Feige
  Department of Economics
  University of Chicago

An Evaluation of Level of Aspiration As a Training Procedure
  Forrest W. Fryer
  Department of Psychology
  University of Maryland

The Measurement of Cumulative Advertising Effects
  Kristian S. Palda
  Graduate School of Business
  University of Chicago

Some Large-Scale Production Scheduling Problems in the Paper Industry
  John F. Pierce, Jr.
  School of Industrial Management
  Massachusetts Institute of Technology

*The Economics of Discretionary Behavior: Managerial Objectives in a
Theory of the Firm*
    Oliver E. Williamson
    Graduate School of Industrial Administration
    Carnegie Institute of Technology

On behalf of the Ford Foundation, I wish to express my gratitude to
the members of the Editorial Committee for the care and thought they
devoted to the selection process. The members of this Committee,
who made the final selection of winning dissertations, were: Professor
Robert Ferber of the University of Illinois, Professor Mason Haire of
the University of California at Berkeley, and Professor Thomas L.
Whisler of the University of Chicago.

The Editorial Committee's task was considerably lightened by the
assistance of twelve readers, experts in the wide range of disciplines
covered in the competition, who carefully screened the theses submitted. The Foundation joins the Committee in acknowledging their
debt to Professors Paul E. Breer of Cornell University, Earl F. Cheit
and Lyman W. Porter of the University of California at Berkeley,
James R. Jackson of the University of California at Los Angeles, Arch
R. Dooley of Harvard University, Daniel M. Holland of the Massachusetts Institute of Technology, Robert J. Holloway of the University
of Minnesota, Donald P. Jacobs of Northwestern University, Bernard
Karsh of the University of Illinois, Walter G. Kell of the University
of Michigan, E. W. Martin, Jr. of Indiana University, and Joseph W.
Newman of Stanford University.

With the publication of these latest winners, the Doctoral Dissertation Competition has completed its planned five-year span. My col-
leagues and I wish to express our appreciation for the generous assistance
which the Ford Foundation has received from many people: Faculty
members too numerous to mention have read and screened the more
than 250 dissertations which have been submitted during the life of the
competition, and Prentice-Hall has contributed its services to the
publicizing and publishing of the selected dissertations.

CLARENCE H. FAUST
VICE PRESIDENT
THE FORD FOUNDATION

New York, N.Y.
January, 1964

Preface

This study grew out of a desire to investigate the extent to which the pattern of investment expenditures on plant and equipment can be explained in terms of the general theory of portfolio balancing and asset allocation. Professor Franco Modigliani (now at Massachusetts Institute of Technology), in a course examining the determinants of macro-economic activity, pointed out that existing explanations of investment expenditure largely ignored the stock-flow relationships which are critical to the investment process, and that no empirical work had been done on examining the links between asset allocation and physical investment.

It was left to Prof. Allan H. Meltzer to suggest that such a study be undertaken. Conceptual insights which provide fundamental foundations for the present study can be found in rudimentary form in Prof. Meltzer's important work on the demand for money.

The bulk of the empirical research on this study was done during the academic year 1961–1962 and the summer of 1962. Virtually all of the calculations were performed on the Bendix G-20 computer operated by the staff of the Computer Center at Carnegie Institute of Technology.

FREDERICK S. HAMMER

ix

Acknowledgments

Assistance toward the completion of this study was received in one form or another from innumerable sources. The debt owed to those unmentioned is at least as great as that which is acknowledged here.

My profound appreciation is extended to my Thesis Committee at Carnegie Institute of Technology, Professors Allan H. Meltzer (Chairman), Kalman J. Cohen, and Dean Richard M. Cyert. Their interest, suggestions, and invariably constructive criticisms advanced far beyond the legitimate responsibilities of Committee membership alone.

For financial support, I am grateful to both the Ford and Danforth Foundations. My last two years as a graduate student were financed by Ford Predoctoral Fellowships, granted by the Foundation as part of their Program in Economic Development and Administration. My first two years were supported by grants from Graduate School of Industrial Administration funds and by Danforth Foundation Fellowships. In addition, I have benefitted greatly under the "relationship of encouragement" extended by the Danforth Foundation. As my understanding and appreciation of the aims of the Foundation matured, this relationship became to me a real and important thing.

Important unpublished data were made available by Dr. Eric Schiff of the Machinery and Allied Products Institute, by Miss Margaret Matulis of the McGraw-Hill Publishing Company, and by Professor Raymond W. Goldsmith and Doctor Robert Lipsey from their forthcoming study at the National Bureau of Economic Research. I am indebted to them for their cooperation.

Mrs. Phyllis L. Conkling typed the final manuscript expertly and with good cheer. Miss Ann Hablow and Miss Bobbie Roper provided helpful clerical assistance.

To my parents, Frederick P. and Rose C. Hammer, go my heartfelt thanks. Their constant encouragement provided tangible support on which the successful completion of my graduate study in large measure depended.

Finally, my greatest debt is to my wife, Ann. Her assistance, steady faith, and refreshing humor made the dissertation not only possible, but a meaningful and worthwhile venture as well.

FREDERICK S. HAMMER

Contents

CHAPTER 1

INTRODUCTION   *1*

CHAPTER 2

PAST APPROACHES AND PROBLEMS   *8*

A.   *Theoretical perspectives*   *8*
B.   *Some problems of validation*   *15*
C.   *Importance to policy considerations*   *19*

CHAPTER 3

THEORETICAL DEVELOPMENT   *25*

A.   *A theory of the firm*   *27*
B.   *The investment equation*   *42*
C.   *Concluding remarks*   *52*

CHAPTER 4

EMPIRICAL TESTS AND IMPLICATIONS OF THE MODEL   *53*

A.   *Measurement of the variables*   *54*
B.   *Statistical findings: 1915–1940, 1946–1961*   *61*
C.   *Short-term considerations*   *78*
D.   *Forecasting investment expenditures*   *86*
E.   *Summary*   *93*

Contents

CHAPTER 5

SYNOPSIS AND IMPLICATIONS   *99*

A.   *The model and evidence: brief review*   *100*
B.   *Theoretical implications of the model*   *105*
C.   *Policy implications*   *110*
D.   *Concluding remarks*   *115*

APPENDIX

THE DATA   *117*

BIBLIOGRAPHY   *129*

CHAPTER 1

Introduction

Recently the United States has been experiencing stern challenges by significant economic developments abroad. Faced with the burgeoning Common Market, the rapid pace of economic progress in the Soviet Union, and the deep concern which the underdeveloped nations are showing for economic growth, many Americans are inspecting with skepticism the underlying structure of their own economic system. The picture they see is indeed a puzzling one. They look to the policy makers for clarification and direction. The policy makers, in turn, seek advice from the experts, who themselves do not agree on a course of action.

The confusion is highlighted by several bills presented in recent years to Congress—bills which aim at stimulating the nation's economy by increased investment in plant and equipment. How to achieve this increased investment has become a main issue of controversy. Various alternatives have been presented, among which are a tax credit, accelerated depreciation, decreased tax rates, increased public expenditures, and an easy monetary policy. None seems to be overwhelmingly popular.

It might appear to the casual onlooker that the problem is merely another partisan squabble. However, on further inspection it becomes more evident that, defying party line, the situation is confused by incomplete understanding of the determinants of capital investment. As one policy maker has said: "The whole problem of instability arising out of plant and equipment is one that is devilishly hard to deal with by public policy."[1]

---

[1] W. W. Heller, Hearings before the Joint Economic Committee on *Employment, Growth and Price Levels*, p. 2997.

This thesis is an attempt to increase our understanding of, and at least in part explain, the pattern of expenditures on plant and equipment by private nonagricultural business in the United States since 1915. There are two essential objectives. *First*, on the theoretical level, we shall attempt to formulate a model of investment expenditures. *Second*, empirical tests will be made in an effort to ascertain the extent to which the model provides useful insights into the critical determinants of investment activity.

Expenditures on plant and equipment by private business have long been recognized as especially ill-understood, considering their importance in the economic system. The widespread concern about these expenditures emanates from three prime sources: (1) the importance of capital expenditures in initiating and/or amplifying fluctuations in the general level of economic activity, (2) their importance in the process of economic growth, an issue which has taken on added significance in recent years, and (3) the implications of capital expenditures for long-term changes in productivity, and thus their effect on standards of living, wage rates, and work habits.

Much work has, of course, been done in this area. For decades, economists have noted that investment expenditures are both highly variable and closely linked to changes in aggregate economic behavior. Illustrating this high correlation are Charts I and II, time series of business investment and gross national product, given in constant and current dollars, respectively.[2] The high variability of the investment series relative to gross national product is further indicated by the coefficients of variation. Using the constant-dollar figures, this statistic is .597 for investment as compared to .475 for GNP. Thus, the relative variability of investment is approximately 25 per cent greater than that of movements in general economic activity. Enticed, therefore, by the obvious relationship between investment and cyclical movements, many investigators have looked for the underlying determinants of investment. Certainly, if these determinants were known, policy making would be simpler.

Some major approaches of previous investigations into the character of investment decisions are examined in Chapter 2. In this discussion, some inadequacies of these previous approaches are noted, as are some

---

[2] The simple correlation coefficient between the investment and gross national product series in constant dollars is .97. The source of the data for gross national product is *U.S. Income and Output, 1958*, U.S. Department of Commerce, and various recent issues of the *Survey of Current Business*. The derivation of the investment data is explained in the Appendix.

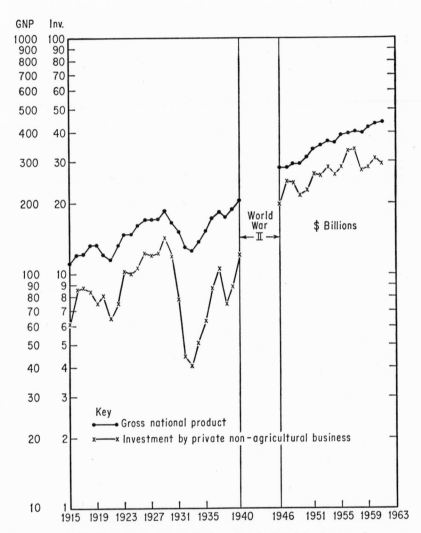

Chart I. Investment by private nonagricultural business and gross national product 1915–1940, 1946–1961. Constant dollars (1954 = 100) (logarithmic scale)

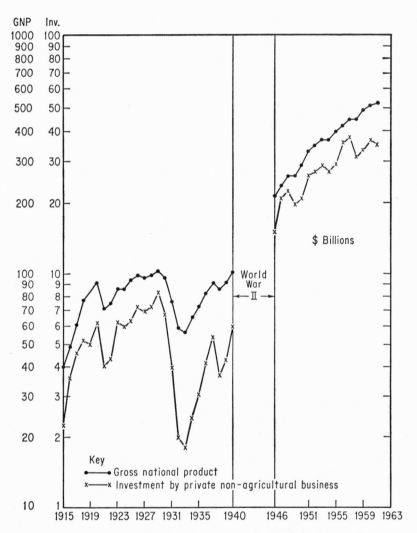

Chart II. Investment by private nonagricultural business and gross national product 1915–1940, 1946–1961. Current dollars (logarithmic scale)

problems which they raise. Consideration is given also to the manner in which the results of research on investment outlays may be expected to influence the policy deliberations of public authorities.

In the substantial amount of work devoted specifically to this topic, some lack of understanding is indicated by the fact that even in models constructed to investigate economic fluctuations—which many theories[3] attribute directly to changes in investment expenditures—the investment variable is sometimes stipulated as exogenous. For example, Duesenberry, Eckstein, and Fromm construct a complex, 14-equation econometric model designed to test the vulnerability of the U.S. economy to recession—and yet take the fixed investment variable as determined from outside the system.[4]

A possible justification for this procedure is that the essential focus of their study was the short-run, transient behavior of the system. Thus, it was not necessary to delineate the endogenous determinants of investment expenditures. However, given the fundamental role that investment plays in business fluctuations and the widespread agreement that these expenditures are significantly affected by transient behavior (e.g., temporary aberrations which might change, say, yield expectations on the one hand and realized profits and wealth on the other), it is certainly not clear that they may be correctly stipulated as exogenous factors. This specification implies that investment is totally caused by "external shocks." Although there may be precedents for this view, it is obvious that, at best, this is an extreme position which would be quite difficult to defend.[5]

An important shortcoming shared by much of the recent theoretical development in the area of capital expenditures is that models designed to explain the investment decision are distinguished more by the emphasis they place on the novel attributes of physical assets than by the common links that underlie the acquisition of all assets. Received models of the investment process (e.g., acceleration and residual funds theories) focus on physical capital alone, thereby ignoring the earnings possibilities and opportunity costs represented by alternative outlets for investment funds. It is clear that physical assets possess some unique properties; it

---

[3] E.g., J. R. Hicks, *A Contribution to the Theory of the Trade Cycle*, Clarendon Press, Oxford, 1950; R. A. Gordon, *Business Fluctuations*, Harper & Row, Publishers, New York, 1952; M. Kalecki, "A Theory of the Business Cycle," *Review of Economic Studies*, 1936, pp. 77–97.

[4] J. S. Duesenberry, O. Eckstein, and G. Fromm, "A Simulation of the United States Economy in Recession," *Econometrica*, 1960, pp. 749–809.

[5] This point is discussed in section A.1, Chapter 2.

is not clear that these idiosyncrasies are of such overwhelming importance that the basic tenets of asset allocation can be overlooked.

In Chapter 3 we develop an investment equation which reflects
both those characteristics which are shared by decisions to acquire any
asset and the unique properties of physical assets. In making explicit
the considerations which underlie asset acquisition, our model of the
firm shows that an optimal asset-liability portfolio depends on both the
firm's wealth and the relative yield of assets, a proposition consistent
with the theory of portfolio balancing. However, the acquisition of (say)
monetary assets differs from that of physical assets in that adjustment
time and transactions costs for money are extremely small relative to the
time and cost of adjusting physical wealth. These special properties of
physical goods must be incorporated into a theory of investment. This
is done in our investment equation by a speed-of-adjustment mechanism
and, later, by adding to investment in any given period the effects produced by the incompleted investment projects of preceding periods.

Another failure of a great proportion of the recent work done on
investment expenditures is that explicit theoretical development of a
hypothesis has not been combined with careful empirical testing of the
model developed. For example, it has been stated, with a certain tone of
resignation, "Our theory of investment is therefore of crucial importance . . . but . . . much of our theory is rather formal and sterile of
empirical content. . . ."[6] To be sure, explanations have been advanced for
this difficulty. The data necessary to test a given hypothesis often are not
available. Sometimes, also, our statistical methodology is not yet far
enough advanced to make adequate tests possible.

Nonetheless, the relative independence of theoretical and empirical
research has led to some unhappy consequences. In particular, in the
absence of prior rigorous development of the hypothesis to be tested,
empirical work is often done in a rather *ad hoc* fashion. For example,
suppose it is desired to test the relation of investment to current profits.
To perform the test, it must first be decided whether profits are to be
used as absolute quantities or, say, as yields on the capital stock. Similarly, should logs or some other transformation of the variables be taken
when making the test? Should price deflators be employed? Should lagged
values of other variables be included? Obviously, a list of such questions
can be extended endlessly.

Without a firm theoretical foundation to guide the empirical effort,
these questions have to be answered arbitrarily. By combining the
theoretical notion with a host of arbitrary procedures, interpretation of

---

[6] G. Ackley, *Macroeconomic Theory*, The Macmillan Company, New York,
1961, p. 460.

the results is rendered tenuous. It is difficult to separate the statistical effects that are inadvertently introduced when making the test from those which are truly indicative of the properties of the theoretical concept. Hence, the usefulness of much empirical work on investment is severely impaired. For the purposes of expanding our understanding of the critical mechanisms underlying decisions to invest, an empirically validated theoretical model is required.

In Chapter 4, a number of empirical tests are made of the investment hypothesis generated by the model of the firm developed in Chapter 3. From the hypothesis and an aggregation procedure, an aggregate demand function for investment in plant and equipment is obtained. Thus, we avoid the errors produced by arbitrarily specifying functional forms and the like. Additional tests of the model are provided by the relative magnitudes of the regression coefficients—another test made possible by explicit theoretical development of the hypothesis.

Besides confusing our understanding of the investment process, empirical tests of investment hypotheses done in an eclectic manner have added greatly to the controversy surrounding policy measures designed to regulate investment expenditures. One salient characteristic of most empirical studies of aggregate business investment has been their unanimity in proclaiming the absence of significant effects exerted by movements in interest rates. This conclusion has been emphasized for two reasons. *First*, it strongly contradicts many of the purely theoretical formulations which characterize the investment literature. *Second*, ability to induce changes in the level of interest rates is one of the primary weapons possessed by monetary policy. Thus, if it is true that monetary policy is ineffectual, public measures to mitigate fluctuations in income inevitably must tend to shift from the monetary to fiscal authorities. Thus, these conclusions contribute to the gradual inflating of fiscal policy as a dominating economic force.

It will be shown below that, from both theoretical and empirical perspectives, interest rates are critical determinants of investment expenditures. When the investment function is formulated in a manner consistent with economic theory, and when empirical tests of this function are specified correctly, the demand for aggregate investment is found to possess a significant interest elasticity. Thus, besides contributing to our understanding of the relationship between investment in physical assets and the general theory of asset acquisition, our results have significant implications for issues of public policy. These implications, along with a review of our procedures and their relationship to prevailing models of investment expenditures are discussed in Chapter 5, with which the study concludes.

CHAPTER 2

Past Approaches and Problems

It is the purpose of this chapter to outline briefly some of the major difficulties facing any inquiry designed to broaden our understanding of the investment process and to indicate some of the approaches utilized by other investigators. It is not our intent to review comprehensively the literature dealing with investment expenditures.[1] We desire here to focus attention on those earlier works which are particularly germane to the present study and to suggest several critical questions to which our results will be shown to have relevance. Accordingly, the major theoretical approaches and some of the problems which they have generated are discussed in section A. Consideration is then transferred to the empirical difficulties involved in validating a model. The chapter concludes with a brief discussion of the relationship between studies of investment expenditures and the relevance of their conclusions for public authorities concerned with the regulation and control of investment activity.

A. Theoretical Perspectives

We can divide the alternative explanations of capital expenditures that have been advanced in the literature into three more or less distinct categories. *First*, there are those stipulating that investment is basically

---

[1] A review of the state of our knowledge on the determinants of business investment has been compiled by R. Eisner, and R. H. Strotz, *Determinants of Business Investment*, Commission on Money and Credit, 1962, especially Chap. 3; also, a thorough tabular summary of the statistical findings obtained by many previous investigators is given by J. R. Meyer, and E. Kuh, *The Investment Decision*, Harvard University Press, Cambridge, Mass., 1957, pp. 23–35.

the result of casual forces which are primarily exogenous to the economic system (e.g., the random discovery of inventions which revolutionize a technological area; wars; etc.). These are represented most notably by the work of Schumpeter.[2] The *second* category is composed of those theories which assert that past or current profits and/or liquidity stocks are the prime motivating factors. The studies by Tinbergen,[3] supported by several later investigations—of which the most influential probably have been those by Klein,[4] Klein and Goldberger,[5] and Meyer and Kuh[6]— are indicative of this approach. *Third*, these are those explanations which invoke alternative specifications of the acceleration principle. Apparently first neatly formulated by Clark,[7] this theory has been impressively extended by, among others, Chenery,[8] Koyck,[9] Modigliani,[10] and Ando.[11]

A1. "Exogenous" Theories. For the purpose of public policy, the theories attributing investment to independent, external forces are of little use. For if it is true that no systematic forces can affect the volume of investment expenditures, then efforts by policy makers to identify and foresee developments which could prove instrumental in altering investment decisions must be, for the most part, haphazard and ineffective. Indeed, to the extent that investment is motivated by forces which are truly random in nature, forecasting attempts must be unsuccessful.

---

[2] J. A. Schumpeter, *Business Cycles: A Theoretical, Historical and Statistical Analysis of the Capitalist Process* (2 vols.), McGraw-Hill, Inc. New York, 1939; also "The Explanation of the Business Cycle," *Economica*, 1927.

[3] J. Tinbergen, *Statistical Testing of Business Cycle Theories*, League of Nations, Geneva, 1938.

[4] L. R. Klein, *Economic Fluctuations in the United States, 1921–1941*, John Wiley & Sons, Inc., New York, 1950.

[5] L. R. Klein and A. S. Goldberger, *An Econometric Model of the United States, 1929–1952*, North-Holland Publishing Company, Amsterdam, 1955.

[6] *Op. cit.*

[7] J. M. Clark, "Business Acceleration and the Law of Demand: A Technical Factor in Economic Cycles," *Journal of Political Economy*, 1917.

[8] H. B. Chenery, "Overcapacity and the Acceleration Principle," *Econometrica*, 1952, pp. 1–28.

[9] L. M. Koyck, *Distributed Lags and Investment Analysis*, North-Holland Publishing Company, Amsterdam, 1954.

[10] F. Modigliani, "Comment," *Problems of Capital Formation*, Studies in Income and Wealth, Vol. 19, National Bureau of Economic Research, New York, 1957, pp. 450–463.

[11] A. K. Ando, *A Contribution to the Theory of Economic Fluctuations and Growth*, unpublished Ph. D. thesis, Carnegie Institute of Technology, April 1959.

In practice, of course, things are not this bleak. Factually, the application of our present theories to the investment problem has shown that we can explain at least some of the movements in capital expenditures. Also, closer reading of the "exogenous theories" indicates that the forces involved may be those motivating *large* secular variations in investment (e.g., that caused by the automobile and its offshoots, the ramifications from which are felt over decades). Thus, for the questions facing policy makers, which are essentially of a shorter-term nature, these theories are viewed as largely irrelevant.[12]

In any event, for the purposes at hand, we will reject this approach. It will be assumed that our understanding of economic mechanisms, while assuredly imperfect, has advanced to the stage where we can formulate hypotheses which will explain at least some portion of the variability in investment expenditures. Indeed, we shall see that, aided by the theory developed in Chapter 3, we are capable of explaining all but an extremely small fraction of this variability.

A2. "Profit" Theories. Two hypotheses have been offered that purport to explain investment in terms of measured current profits. The

---

[12] The one issue for which the "exogenous theories," if correct, could have a large importance for measuring the possible effectiveness of policy measures is that of long-term secular growth. If it is true that long-term movements can be stimulated only by exogenous forces, and if it is impossible to identify and foster these forces beforehand, then any efforts made by the authorities to quicken the growth rate will obviously be ineffectual.

It is the perspective of this study that policies undertaken by the monetary and fiscal authorities do, in fact, affect the growth rate. The feedback effects of investment on demand via the multiplier illustrate at least one avenue by which successful efforts to stimulate the level of capital expenditures will influence the rate of output and, thus, growth.

Also, it is by no means clear that "exogenous theories" are to be accepted on any count. In this connection, it is interesting to note that the Schumpeterian argument, i.e., that the central causes of business cycles are major technical innovations, has lately come under attack. J. Schmookler has arrayed impressive evidence that innovations themselves are significantly affected by the state of economic conditions and, thus, cannot be properly understood as "autonomous shocks" to the system. While the conclusions and the accompanying investigative procedures are almost certain to be criticized (e.g., the measurement of innovations by the number of patents granted), the results should at least render doubtful the acceptance of the "shock" approach. (Cf. J. Schmookler, "Invention, Innovation, and Business Cycles," in *Variability of Private Investment in Plant and Equipment*, Part II, Washington, D. C., 1962). Additional work on investment in innovations has recently been reported by E. Mansfield, in "Entry, Gibrat's Law, Innovation, and the Growth of Firms," *American Economic Review*, 1962, pp. 1023–1051, and "Technical Change and the Rate of Imitation," *Econometrica*, 1961, pp. 741–766.

first, the "expected profits hypothesis," asserts that current profits are a good surrogate for expected future profits, and since it is the latter that govern investment expenditures, the former may be used as an appropriate explanatory variable. Actually, it is by no means clear that present realizations accurately measure expectations of the future. In addition, costs (interest expenses, the prices of machinery, etc.) are not explicitly introduced into this framework, although certainly changes in costs will have immediate repercussions on the expected profits, and thus on investment. Finally, the "profits" equations tested have never been derived from models incorporating all the root assumptions which the researcher attributes to the final equation. Klein is quite explicit about this point. After spending an entire chapter developing the theory underlying economic decisions, he then includes an investment equation in which absolute profits enter as an explanatory variable—*counter* to the theoretical considerations. His justification for this procedure is that the "equation expresses the heuristic principle, that profits are the mainspring of economic action in a capitalist society."[13]

Certainly heuristics have an important place in the development of our understanding. Nor do we question here the prime importance of profits as the "mainspring" behind investment expenditures in a market economy. But heuristics are dangerous in one very important regard, for while one's intuition may well indicate fruitful paths to investigate, it is at least equally probable that loose ends will be left unless the theoretical foundations underlying one's "hunch" are at some time carefully structured and evaluated.[14]

In the present case, for instance, the question is raised, should profits enter the investment equation as absolute quantities or as the *yields* on capital, or assets, or investment? If entered in erroneous form, when viewed from the perspective of the "true" model, might it not be that the success indicated is due not to the attributes of the profits variable itself, but to other variables whose true structural effects are statistically mirrored in our measures of profits? Indeed, both Eisner[15]

---

[13] Klein, *op. cit.* (1950).

[14] An attempt by Klein in a later paper to justify his inclusion of absolute profits in the investment equation is regarded as antithetical to his original assumption of profit maximization by Eisner and Strotz, *op. cit.*, Chap. 1.

[15] R. Eisner, "Capital Expenditures, Profits and the Acceleration Principle," preliminary version given at the Conference on Research in Income and Wealth, Feb. 2, 3, 1962, National Bureau of Economic Research; also, "Expectations, Plans, and Capital Expenditures: A Synthesis of Ex Post and Ex Ante Data," in *Expectations, Uncertainty and Business Behavior*, Social Science Research Council, M. J. Bowman, ed., pp. 49–58,

and Grunfeld[16] have argued forcefully that profits serve merely as a "proxy" for other variables and should not be included themselves, *per se*, as an explanatory variable in investment relations.

In the more inclusive theoretical structure to be offered below, *viz.*, the wealth model, profits enter the investment equation as the yields on assets. Thus, this model allows immediate attention to be focused at the heart of the issue—on assets themselves. The investment equation is a direct outgrowth of the model depicting the situation in which the firm makes its decisions. The functional specification of, and the form in which the variables enter, the investment equation are not subject to later, hypertheoretical considerations. We will return to these points below.

The *second* attempted explanation of investment in terms of the profits variable concentrates on the role of profits in maintaining an adequate liquidity position for the firm. Investment will supposedly be undertaken only when enough liquid assets are possessed to finance expenditures (or some preassigned portion) from the funds internally held. Often borrowing is eschewed and interest costs are not considered. This approach appears to have gained its most articulate foundation in the study made by Meyer and Kuh, where it emerges with the name of the "residual funds hypothesis."

The seeds of this residual fund hypothesis seem to have been planted by Berle and Means in their classic study.[17] Their observation that management and ownership had become separated led to the conclusion that, since management had been placed in a position which allowed them to ignore the stockholders' desire for large dividends, more emphasis would be placed on retained earnings and other internally generated funds to finance the corporation's activities. Consequently, the need to resort to external funds would largely disappear.

Evidence for this conclusion has not been forthcoming. In Lintner's analysis of the sources from which corporations have obtained their funds in this century, he states: "The conclusion seems inescapable that there has been no secular net change in the relative dependence of internal funds to expand assets among all nonfinancial corporations over this broad sweep of time."[18] Also, in reviewing the evidence pertaining to

    [16] Y. Grunfeld, "The Determinants of Capital Investment," in *The Demand for Durable Goods*, A. C. Harberger, ed., University of Chicago Press, Chicago, 1960, pp. 211–266.

    [17] A. A. Berle, Jr., and G. C. Means, *The Modern Corporation and Private Property*, The Macmillan Company, New York, 1934.

    [18] J. Lintner, "The Financing of Corporations," pp. 166–201 in *The Corporation in Modern Society*, E. A. Mason, ed., Harvard University Press, Cambridge, Mass., 1961, p. 181.

Berle and Means' thesis that the corporation would become essentially independent of outside capital markets, Lintner concludes: " . . . these markets continue to be major sources of capital to finance business expansion, and any assertion that corporations are no longer dependent upon them for an important part of such financing is sheer exaggeration."[19]

It is worth remarking in this connection that the major evidence of residual funds hypothesis, *viz.*, that secured by Meyer and Kuh, is based on data from the five years 1946–1950. However, because of the huge stocks of liquid assets that had been accumulated during World War II, we would expect that the need to resort to outside funds to finance investment outlays would be negligible during the years in the immediate postwar period. In addition, it should be remembered that during this period interest rates were artificially low, owing to the policy of the Federal Reserve System to support bond prices at high levels. Since only low yields could be earned on alternative placement of funds, there was little motivation on the part of corporate treasurers to economize cash balances.[20] Thus, any conclusion based on evidence acquired for this period cannot be legitimately broadened to encompass other periods in which the financial environment is less benign.[21]

The "profit" hypotheses have been criticized both for statistical reasons[22] and on grounds that the economic justification is faulty.[23] But what appears to be the more devastating criticism of this approach is the simple realization that even a firm making low or negative profits may well be confronted with an opportunity that will earn for it future profits. Only in a world with the most gross imperfections in its financial

---

[19] *Ibid.*, p. 185.

[20] This point has been recognized by A. H. Meltzer, in "The Demand for Money: The Evidence from the Time Series," *Journal of Political Economy*, June 1963, pp. 219–246. He writes: "In a regime of price controls, it would be surprising to find the price ratios equal to the marginal rates of substitution between commodities. The effect of price controls is to distort observed economic relationships. Similar results undoubtedly hold for bond price controls or pegged interest rates" (p. 242).

[21] The experience of recent years supports this statement. As noted by Hauge, "The disappointing rate of new investment since 1956 should have exploded the fallacy that since 'cash flow' has risen, nothing specific need be done to increase the profitability of investment. For cash flow—depreciation reserves plus retained earnings—has clearly trended up, while investment has not." G. Hauge, "Economic Growth: An American View," pp. 21–34 in *Economic Growth—Balance of Payments*, The American Bankers Association, 1962, p. 25.

[22] T. Haavelmo, "The Effect of the Rate of Interest on Investment: A Note," *Review of Economic Statistics*, 1947, pp. 49–52.

[23] R. Eisner, "A Distributed Lag Investment Function," *Econometrica*, 1960, pp. 1–30.

markets will this firm be denied the funds it needs to undertake the relevant investment. Yet investment under these circumstances is not possible under the residual funds hypothesis. If profits are low and liquid assets, thereby, are at a minimum, investment is precluded, or, at least, outside the model.

This "explanation" is not very satisfying. Indeed, for some firms it may make more sense to argue from a directly opposite position, i.e., that the prime motivation to invest comes from a *loss* of profits rather than from high profits. A loss of profits, especially relative to one's competitors or when accompanied by declining sales or an eroding away of market share, may cause the firm to initiate projects in an effort to regain, and possibly improve upon, its former position. At a minimum, this would suggest that the profit relation is not single valued.[24]

A3. "Accelerator" Theories. Perhaps the simplest version of the "accelerator" theories is one in which a firm's desired stock of capital is taken as proportional to its output. Investment, which is usually taken as a fraction of the difference between the desired and actual stock of capital, is thus a linear function of output during a given period. The major limitations of this theory are that (1) it is inapplicable when output is falling and the called-for rate of disinvestment is greater than the actual rate of capital consumption, and (2) investment may take place even in the absence of rising output because of desires to increase efficiency, decrease unit costs, improve profit position, etc.[25] These shortcomings have been noted by many authors, and there have been abundant attempts to modify the theory to correct the weaknesses. For our purposes, it is interesting to note that while the residual funds hypothesis centers on past profits' being permissive, the acceleration hypothesis

---

[24] Thus, for example, March and Simon "predict efforts toward innovation in a company whose share of market, total profits, or rate of return on investment had declined" (p. 183). Obviously, one form which this innovation might be expected to take is investment in plant and equipment needed for improving quality, new products, etc. (Cf. J. G. March and H. A. Simon, *Organizations*, Prentice-Hall, Inc., Englewood Cliffs, N. J., 1958.)

[25] A unique criticism has been launched against the accelerator models in the recent book by V. L. Smith, *Investment and Production*, Harvard University Press, Cambridge, Mass., 1961. Smith argues that "By using a Cobb-Douglas production function it is shown that investment is a decreasing or increasing function of the level of output according to whether the process shows increasing or decreasing returns to scale" (p. 18). He concludes: "If there is anything to the widely held view that most manufacturing processes exhibit increasing returns to scale, it could well mean that the aggregate investment demand function is a decreasing function of the level of output" (p. 318). Thus, Smith's conclusion is directly contrary to the fundamental postulate of the acceleration principle.

may be interpreted as motivating investment only in the pursuit of expected profits, or, at least, in order to increase the probability of enhancing earnings potential.

The acceleration hypotheses are thus similar to the expected profits hypothesis in using current measures as a surrogate for expected future conditions. Those utilizing the acceleration principle have often measured these expectations in terms of current levels of sales. When capacity becomes insufficient for the firm to supply its customers, expansion of the capital stock is desired and investment is undertaken. A constant capital coefficient (which is in itself questionable) is introduced, thereby enabling the investigator to obtain a measure of present capacity by utilizing the value of fixed plant and equipment.

Although results forthcoming from this approach have occasionally been encouraging, the potential that has always been promised seems never to be reached. For example, while Chenery's model[26] was quite successful in some industries, the results were abysmal when it was applied to others with supposedly similar characteristics. Similarly, while the sophisticated version of this principle derived by Ando[27] is stimulating theoretically, his attempts at empirical validation were decidedly negative. Ando attributes these results to the imperfect data available with which to make the tests. However, data are never of the quality we would like, and it appears sterile to support one's contentions on the basis of evidence which does not exist.

Notwithstanding all these criticisms, the explanations of investment obtained from the accelerator models are by far the most popular. It is the position of the present study that these accelerator models are a special case of the wealth model utilized here. The key variables in the accelerator formulation, *viz.*, sales and capital, can be interpreted in terms of the wealth model. Measures of capital stock, of course, are closely correlated with measures of wealth, and just as profits can be interpreted as a net yield, sales may be interpreted as gross yield on assets.

B. Some Problems of Validation

In our attempt to empirically validate a given model, two key problems that must be solved are (1) how to measure the variables that are required by the theoretical considerations, and (2) selection of the time period from which to select the data to be used. Since these problems

---

[26] *Op. cit.*
[27] *Op. cit.*

were quite important in dictating the scope of the tests made on the model of the present study, it is appropriate to consider some of the salient issues which these problems involve.

B1. Measurement of the Variables. In reviewing the profits and acceleration approaches we note that, in both, some measure of expectations is required to specify the models. One of the shortcomings of previous tests of these models—which is not to be confused with shortcomings in the models *per se*—has been the failure to measure expectations in a satisfactory manner.

Grunfeld,[28] in his study of the capital expenditures of eight individual firms, introduced the market value of the firm—an apparently new consideration in the investment literature—as the prime determinant of the firm's desired stock of capital. Grunfeld interprets the variable as including both expectations and the cost of capital, and indicates that these effects are essentially separable. His results are encouraging, given the small sample of firms he studied, and the market value variable should be a prominent candidate for any tentative investment model. Of course, since the market value of the shares of the firm measures the worth of the firm viewed by essentially objective, unbiased investors, this variable is a measure of the wealth of the firm. Indeed, economic theory specifies that wealth is the capitalized value of one's future earnings. This is precisely the interpretation which we will give to the market value of the firm.

A second variable of critical importance to investment theories is the capital stock, measurement of which has continually baffled economists.[29] The problems in this connection are varied and complex, and it does not appear fruitful to review them here. Tests of the accelerator

---

[28] *Op. cit.*

[29] See, e.g., J. Robinson, "The Production Function and the Theory of Capital," *Review of Economic Studies*, 1953–54. While Mrs. Robinson carefully points out the problems of measuring the stock of capital, given the classical economic concept of what this measure should be, Simon points out that the value of the capital stock cannot be measured independently of a measure valuing the ability of the work force to utilize this stock. This raises a host of subsidiary issues which are devastating to the classical concepts. (H. A. Simon, "Decision Making as an Economic Resource," forthcoming.) Illustrative of the attempts to solve some of these problems are articles by Solow, on a theoretical level, and by Dennison on a practical level. (Cf. R. M. Solow, "The Production Function and the Theory of Capital," *Review of Economic Studies*, 1955–56, pp. 101–108, and E. F. Dennison, "Problems in Theory of Capital," in Studies in Income and Wealth, Vol. 19, *op. cit.*) Also relevant is the important article by A. P. Lerner, "On the Marginal Product of Capital and the Marginal Efficiency of Investment," *Journal of Political Economy*, 1953, pp. 1–14.

theories have been particularly impaired by our inability to measure this and related variables (e.g., the capacity to produce); it shall be seen below that one of the weaknesses in the validation of the present model arises from this same inability.

B2. Time Span. A large proportion of the investment literature concentrates on short-term, cross-section investigations. They center on variables, such as liquidity, sales, and enunciated, *ex ante* anticipations. These have often not incorporated any explicit theoretical framework, but have been experimental in nature and primarily directed toward specifying "determinants," which appear to be defined as variables that significantly (in the statistical sense) correlate with measures of investment expenditures. In the case of anticipations data, much of the effort appears to have been expended in testing the degree of reliability which may be accorded the anticipations as harbingers of actual performance[30]

The relative lack of long-term studies of investment behavior may be explained by two considerations. First, the data leave much to be desired, both in duration and in quality. The Department of Commerce series begins only in 1929, and the Securities and Exchange Commission-Federal Trade Commission series begins as recently as 1945. Thus, it is only in recent years that enough observations have become available to make the contemplated results of any such study seem at all worthwhile.

This difficulty is compounded by the fact that the data on relevant variables, such as capital consumption (as measured, say, by real depreciation flows), market value of the capital stock, and degree of utilization of capacity—to mention but a few—have not been readily available in the past. Nor, indeed, are they totally available now, although some attempts have recently been made to compile the esti-

---

[30] E.g., I. Friend and J. Bronfenbrenner, "Business Investment Programs and Their Realizations," *Survey of Current Business*, December 1950, pp. 11–22; D. M. Keezer, *et al.*, "Observations on the Predictive Quality of McGraw-Hill Surveys of Business' Plans for New Plants and Equipment" in *The Quality and Economic Significance of Anticipations Data*, National Bureau of Economic Research, New York, 1960, pp. 369–385; R. Ferber, "Measuring the Accuracy and Structure of Businessmen's Expectations," *Journal of the American Statistical Association*, 1953, pp. 385–413; F. Modigliani and H. M. Weingartner, "Forecasting Uses of Anticipatory Data on Investment and Sales," *Quarterly Journal of Economics*, 1958, pp. 23–54; A. M. Okun, "The Value of Anticipations Data in Forecasting National Product," pp. 407–451 in the *Quality and Significance of Anticipations Data*, N.B.E.R., *op. cit.*; A. M. Okun, "The Predictive Value of Surveys of Business Intentions," *The American Economic Review*, May 1962, pp. 218–225.

mates of some of the measures. The recently published study by Gold-smith[31] has also helped to make inroads on the data problem. But, for the most part, historical data on the variables called for by theoretical considerations inevitably have had to be estimated from imperfect, related information which is available. Resort to this approach was necessary in this study also.[32]

Second, there apparently exists a current of opinion holding that the structure of the system underlying the investment relation has changed over time. Proper reasons may be advanced for excluding the war years on the grounds that normal allocative patterns and decision-making procedures were so disrupted because of the war effort that businessmen were forced to change their habits drastically. The presence of price controls, priorities in the use of materials, and other restrictions intro-duced elements which distort optimizing behavior in a market economy. The efficiency of the pricing system is reduced when plans for allocating resources are imposed from above. Hence, decisions on investment out-lays during these years will be motivated by forces which are different from those operating in the absence of wartime controls.[33]

Similarly, an argument can be made that the development of tech-nical tools and managerial sophistication has so changed the basis on which decisions are made—investment decision included—that the years prior to the war should be excluded. Tax laws, amortization schedules, arrangements in financial markets—all these have changed since the prewar period. Again, the postwar boom and the years of the Korean crisis appear atypical and, too, are excluded. The argument then requires that we begin our study in 1953 or so. But the degrees of freedom left, after so curtailing the number of observations to be investigated, are too small to allow the study to be of any interest. Thus, the time series approach is often abandoned.

It is by no means clear that the past should be shrugged off so cav-alierly. *First,* we do not have access to so much information that we can ignore a large part of our experience when dealing with problems as complex as that being examined here. *Second,* once the rationality hypothesis (or a variant thereof) is invoked, it is a short next step to assert that while the availability of new tools, changes in institutional setting, and other factors may change decision-making procedures, the very presence of the basic tendency to seek a maximizing equilibrium

----

[31] R. W. Goldsmith, *A Study of Savings in the United States* (3 vols.), Princeton University Press, Princeton, N. J., 1953.

[32] The data and methods of computation used in this study are contained in the Appendix.

[33] Cf. March and Simon, *Organizations, op. cit.,* pp. 200–208.

point should allow the "best way" to have been approached over time. Identification of the relevant functions would thus seem to be enhanced by including as many years as possible in the time span investigated. *Third,* there is an impressive collection of studies indicating that the structure of basic economic relations is indeed relatively constant over time, i.e., movements in the dependent variable can be taken as movements along the function as against a shift of the function itself.[34] *Finally,* it should be noted that the statement that the demand function for capital has changed over time is an hypothesis about economic behavior and as such is capable of denial based on evidence.[35] Thus, it was decided that the battery of tests to which the model of the succeeding chapter would be subjected in the present study would be of a time series nature.

C. Importance to Policy Considerations

The results of investigations into the factors underlying the decision to invest are important in shaping the character of future actions taken by the policy-making authorities when attempting to affect the rate of investment in business plant and equipment. For example, if a residual funds hypothesis is adopted, a decrease in the tax rate on corporate profits would, in itself, be taken as sufficient to stimulate investment. Under an accelerator explanation, it would also be necessary to trace the probable effects of this action to ascertain whether such a decrease would then stimulate demand and output, the principal determinant of investment of this latter class of hypotheses.

Of more significance, however, is the question whether primary reliance should be placed on monetary or on fiscal policy when dealing with desired changes in the volume of investment expenditures. Naively,

---

[34] E.g., P. Cagan, "The Monetary Dynamics of Hyperinflation," in *Studies in the Quantity Theory of Money,* M. Friedman, ed., University of Chicago Press, Chicago, 1956, pp. 25–117. Investigation of the demand for real cash balances shows that one equation is sufficient to explain the preponderance of variability in this series during seven hyperinflations in six different countries—hardly a situation in which, *a priori,* one would expect constant structure to exist. Similarly, Meltzer, *op. cit.,* shows that the demand for money in the United States during the years 1900–1958 can be virtually completely explained in terms of a single, constant equation. These same implications can, of course, be drawn from the work on the consumption function by Friedman. (Cf. M. Friedman, *A Theory of the Consumption Function,* National Bureau of Economic Research, New York, 1957.)

[35] The functional stability of the investment equation implied by the theory of the firm presented in the succeeding chapter is subjected to empirical test in Chapter 4.

we may view this issue as one between the "interventionists" (i.e., the advocates of fiscal policy), on the one hand, and the "noninterventionists" (i.e., those who favor monetary policy), on the other. The rationale for this dichotomy resides in the fact that the use of fiscal tools (e.g., interjecting an autonomous source of demand) essentially implies an *alteration* of the structure of the system in which firms operate and formulate their decisions, while the techniques of monetary policy are primarily designed to affect movements along the supply schedule of available funds, and thereby exert their forces *within* a fundamentally stable structural system. Thus, while fiscal measures require policy decisions of the kind that directly affect investment, monetary policy permits this ultimate decision to remain in the hands of the individual economic unit and attempts to influence the genre of the decision being made.

The methods by which the monetary authorities seek to affect the volume of funds available to firms are usually thought to exert influence on investment decisions through their effects on the *cost* of these funds, given by the rate of interest.[36] Thus, one important method of testing whether or not monetary policy is an effective route by which to influence investment is to investigate the relationship between interest rates and the volume of these expenditures. Past efforts in this direction have been puzzlingly negative.

Nowhere in the models tested successfully in the literature does there enter an explicit cost variable. The closest approximation is Grunfeld's interest rate, but this is buried in his market value variable. From a theoretical perspective, this is somewhat disturbing. All theories of capital budgeting require some notion of capital costs to enter into consideration when attempting to define the cut-off point for the investment opportunities that should be undertaken by a firm.[37]

----

[36] It is often argued that the primary effect of monetary operations in influencing investment is not through interest costs, but through the forces they exert in changing the volume of funds available. However, funds are always available at *some* cost, however high, if only the potential borrower is willing to offer these rates.

Also, there exists a large assortment of observable interest rates which correspond to the varied types and maturities of available funds. Since different classes of funds are relevant to the different kinds of investment decisions which occur, it is difficult to obtain a single, satisfactory measure which will adequately describe the level of interest rates for all relevant classes of funds. Thus, we encounter another problem of measurement similar to those mentioned in the preceding section. How serious this problem is will depend on the correlations between the various rates of interest.

[37] E.g., F. A. Lutz and V. C. Lutz, *The Theory of Investment of the Firm*, Princeton University Press, Princeton, N. J., 1951; I. Fisher, *Theory of Interest*, 1930; H. Bierman and S. Schmidt, *The Capital Budgeting Decision*, The Macmillan Company, New York, 1960.

It appears that three problems have been encountered in attempts to establish the importance of variables which measure capital costs. *First*, there is the disrepute into which the role of interest rates fell after the survey studies in this country and the United Kingdom.[38] *Second*, empirical work has indicated that regression coefficients for interest rate variables are usually not only statistically insignificant, but of the wrong sign as well.[39] *Third*, several plausible theoretical reasons have been advanced why interest rates will not enter into profitability calculations, and, thus, why the marginal efficiency of capital schedule is interest-inelastic.[40]

However, recent thinking leads one to question the validity of these results. *First*, recent research on the procedures utilized in the survey studies has indicated that the results obtained by these studies must be regarded quite reservedly. One observer has concluded that "In view of all their defects, no definite conclusion can be drawn from the surveys of business attitudes toward capital costs."[41]

Second, inspection of the methods employed in the empirical investigations of the effects of interest rates on investment, leads one to doubt the reliability of these results also. In particular, it is not clear that the variables employed, purporting to measure interest costs, have been entered into the hypothesis in a theoretically defensible manner. It appears that in virtually all statistical tests of the significance of interest rates, the hypothesis tested was an eclectic one, in which variables selected "seemed" to be relevant, and for which no complete underlying model had been constructed. Thus, in these tests no attempt was made to examine the form of the variables or functional specification of the hy-

[38] E.g., P. W. S. Andrews and E. Brunner, *Capital Development in Steel: A Study of the United Steel Companies, Ltd.*, Oxford University Press, London, 1951; P. W. S. Andrews, "A Further Inquiry into the Effects of Rates of Interest," *Oxford Economic Papers*, 1940, pp. 33–73; W. W. Heller, "The Anatomy of Investment Decisions," *Harvard Business Review*, 1951, pp. 95–103; J. F. Ebersole, "The Influence of Interest Rates Upon Entrepreneurial Decisions in Business—A Case Study," *Harvard Business Review*, Autumn 1938, pp. 35–40; J. E. Meade and P. W. S. Andrews, "Summary of Replies to Questions on Effects of Interest Rates," *Oxford Economic Papers*, 1938, pp. 14–31.

[39] See, e.g., the works by Tinbergen, Meyer, and Kuh, and Klein and Goldberger, cited above. Similar results are reported by A. Kisselgoff and F. Modigliani, "Private Investment in the Electric Power Industry and the Acceleration Principle," *Review of Economics and Statistics*, 1957, pp. 363–379.

[40] E.g., R. Eisner, "Interview and Other Survey Techniques and the Study of Investment," pp. 513–584 in *Problems of Capital Formation*, N.B.E.R., 1957, *op. cit.*

[41] W. H. White, "Interest Inelasticity of Investment Demand—The Case from Business Attitude Surveys Examined," pp. 565–587 in *American Economic Review*, 1956, p. 587. White's work is extended in his "The Changing Criteria in Investment Planning," pp. 1–24 of the *Variability of Private Investment*, Part II, *op. cit.*

pothesis. Variables are tested in various combinations, and linear relationships are utilized because of their statistical convenience. Surely no firm conclusions can be based on these fundamentally unsystematic experiments.[42] In addition, it is possible that a negative bias is introduced in the tests of significance for the effects of interest rates on investment by the presence of errors in measurement of the interest rate variable.[43]

---

[42] Of course, arbitrary specification of such functional forms as linear is understandable in the interests of simplicity and in view of the state of our statistical methodology. Indeed, when working with large simultaneous systems, as does Klein in his pioneering works, no other recourse is practical at present. But the specification is still arbitrary, and the nonsignificance of certain variables (e.g., interest rates in Klein's investment equation) in the equations tested cannot be taken as proof that those variables are unrelated to the question at issue, but only that the form tested failed to show this relationship. This elementary point appears to have been ignored by many of those viewing the results of research which incorporate such arbitrary specifications.

[43] Suppose one is attempting to ascertain the statistical significance of the relationship between Y and X, which we observe with no errors in measurement. Measuring both variables from their mean, the model is

$$Y = \alpha X + u,$$

where u is normally and independently distributed with constant, finite variance and zero mean. Our estimate of the parameter α is

$$\hat{\alpha} = \frac{\text{Cov }(X, Y)}{.\text{Var }(X)},$$

where

$$P \lim (\hat{\alpha}) = \alpha.$$

The standard error of this estimate is

$$\sigma_{\hat{\alpha}} = \left[\frac{\text{Var }(u)}{n \text{ Var }(X)} \right]^{1/2}.$$

Thus, our measure of statistical significance of the relationship (i.e., of $\hat{\alpha}$) is

$$t = \frac{\hat{\alpha}}{\sigma_{\hat{\alpha}}} = \frac{\dfrac{\text{Cov }(X, Y)}{\text{Var }(X)}}{\left[\dfrac{\text{Var }(u)}{n \text{ Var }(X)} \right]^{1/2}} = \frac{\sqrt{n} \text{ Cov }(X, Y)}{[\text{Var }(X) \text{ Var }(u)]^{1/2}}.$$

Suppose now that there are measurement errors in our observation of the independent variable X. Thus, instead of observing X, we observe $x = X - v$, where v is the error of measurement. We make the conventional assumptions that

(i) $E(v) = E(vX) = E(vY) = E(uv) = 0,$ $E(v^2) = k.$

Our model then becomes

$$Y = \alpha X + u = \alpha x + \alpha v + u$$

or

$$Y = \alpha x + w,$$

where

$$w = \alpha v + u$$

and the following relationships hold:

$$\text{Var } (x) = \text{Var } (X) + \text{Var } (v),$$

$$\text{Var } (w) = \text{Var } (u) + \alpha^2 \text{Var } (v),$$

$$\text{Cov } (x, Y) = \text{Cov } (X, Y).$$

Utilizing the observations on Y and x, the estimate of α is

$$\hat{\alpha}^0 = \frac{\text{Cov } (x, y)}{\text{Var } (x)} = \frac{\text{Cov } (X, Y)}{\text{Var } (X) + \text{Var } (v)} < \hat{\alpha}.$$

Thus, as is well known, the estimate of the regression coefficient is biased downward when errors of measurement are present. The standard error of $\hat{\alpha}^0$ is

$$\sigma_{\hat{\alpha}^0} = \left[\frac{\text{Var } (w)}{n \text{ Var } (x)} \right]^{1/2} = \left[\frac{\alpha^2 \text{Var } (v) + \text{Var } (u)}{n \text{ Var } (X) + n \text{ Var } (v)} \right]^{1/2}.$$

The t-statistic, which is used to test the statistical significance of $\hat{\alpha}^0$, is

$$t^0 = \frac{\hat{\alpha}^0}{\sigma_{\hat{\alpha}^0}}$$

$$= \frac{[\sqrt{n} \text{ Cov } (X, Y)]}{\{\text{Var } (X) \text{ Var } (u) + [\alpha^2 \text{ Var } (v) \text{ Var } (X) + \alpha^2 \text{ Var } (v)^2 + \text{Var } (u) \text{ Var } (v)]\}^{1/2}}.$$

Inspection of t and t^0 reveals that while their numerators are identical, the denominator of t^0 is larger than that of t, owing to the presence of the terms in the square brackets. Therefore, $|t| > |t^0|$, from which we conclude that the presence of errors of measurement in the independent variable results in a downward bias in the statistical tests of significance for the regression coefficient of the independent variable.

This analysis suggests that to the extent that errors are present in the available measures of interest rates which possess the properties indicated in (i) above, tests of significance for interest rate effects on investment will be downward biased.

Undoubtedly some errors of measurement do exist. Interest costs depend on bank loan rates, compensating balance requirements, the level of bond prices, various restrictions tied to the particular characteristics of projects for which funds are sought, etc. On the other hand, our measures of interest costs are usually taken from indices of yields on long-term Government issues or high-grade corporate bonds. To the extent that such measures abstract from the costs inherent in particular classes of loans, errors of measurement are introduced. Of course, insofar as these measurement errors are proportional to reported rates, it can be shown that the statistical significance of estimated regression coefficients will be unaffected in spite of the fact that the estimates of the coefficients themselves remain biased.

Thus, in testing for the effects of interest rates on investment, statistical problems are raised by our measurement procedures. We do not take this problem as the major source of statistical difficulty; on the contrary, that distinction is reserved for errors of specification which have pervaded previous tests, as discussed above. Nonetheless, the presence of measurement errors does militate against the gathering of conclusive evidence.

Third, on the theoretical level, Tarshis[44] has shown that the reasons advanced to explain away the importance of interest rates to the marginal efficiency function are themselves, when subjected to careful scrutiny, founded on quite tenuous foundations. Capital costs, when correctly specified and correctly entered into the model, should, on both theoretical and intuitive grounds, be of importance in an investment function.

In the following chapter, we shall develop an investment relation derived from a model of the firm based directly on motivational and environmental assumptions. We shall find that the hypothesis implies that interest rates do indeed play a significant role in this equation. In Chapter 4, this equation is subjected to a number of empirical tests which, among other things, afford us an opportunity to determine whether or not interest costs do, in fact, exert a significant effect on the rate of investment.

---

[44] L. Tarshis, "The Elasticity of the Marginal Efficiency Function," *American Economic Review*, 1961, pp. 958–985, and "Comments" by O. E. Williamson and L. Abbott, 1962, pp. 1099–1110.

CHAPTER 3

Theoretical Development

One of the major conclusions of the preceding discussion is that in the past there have been very few attempts to formulate a model of investment based on an explicitly developed theory of the firm. It was argued that this approach, which we have termed eclectic, is subject to grave deficiencies in at least two respects: *first*, the form of the investment relation tested cannot be uniquely established, and *second*, unambiguous interpretation of empirical results is virtually impossible in the absence of a supporting theoretical structure.

The model of investment derived in this chapter is dominated by one major theoretical consideration: that investment in a given asset is the result of a decision to change the actual stock of that asset to a given desired level. Such a decision will be made when the actual and desired stocks of the asset differ. Thus, apart from problems which arise in measuring the actual stock, the key theoretical issue which must be examined lies in the determination of the underlying factors on which the desired stock depends.

The traditional, neoclassic theory of the firm is thus subject to limitation in the area of capital investment. In that theory, emphasis is placed on the *flows* of factor inputs and product outputs, and the only consideration given to the role of the firm's *stock* positions is buried in the production function.[1] Consequently, additional theory, in which emphasis is shifted from flows to stocks, is needed for study of the investment decision.[2]

The wealth model of the firm presented below allows a new perspective to be brought to the theory of the firm. Entrepreneurial motivation remains consistent with that assumed in the traditional theory, i.e., it is desired to maximize profits. But while in traditional theory the profits function is formulated as the difference between revenues and costs defined in terms of units produced, in the present model profits are viewed as the difference between the yields on *stocks* of assets and the rate of payments emanating from *stocks* of liabilities. Also, the firm's (stock of) wealth replaces the production function as the constraint with respect to which the profits function is maximized. Attention is thereby directly focused on the causal factors governing the desired stock of an asset. An empirically testable investment equation is immediately implied. Having been derived in this manner, the form of the equation and its variables are precisely specified, and the attendant assumptions necessary to the derivation are explicitly identified. Interpretation of the empirical results of Chapter 4 is thereby clarified.

The change in orientation from traditional theory to the present model is a simple result of the change in the kind of question the theory is designed to answer. A basic question asked by the traditional theory

---

[1] See, for example, P. A. Samuelson, *Foundations of Economic Analysis*, Harvard University Press, Cambridge, Mass., 1947, Chap. 4, or J. R. Hicks, *Value and Capital*, Oxford University Press, London, 2nd ed., 1946, esp. Part II and corresponding mathematical appendices. An interpretation of the traditional theory of the firm which differs slightly from that given by Hicks is contained in "The Analogy Between Producer and Consumer Equilibrium Analysis" (Part I, "Outline of the Problem and Conclusions," by H. Makower, and Part II, "Income Effect, Substitution Effect, Ricardo Effect," by W. J. Baumol), *Economica*, 1950, pp. 63–80. It is of interest to note that Makower, in Part I of this article, defines the budget constraint as the sum of initial endowments (exactly as is done in the theory of exchange), thereby eliminating the possibility of borrowing. Baumol is more general in that the budget constraint includes the amount of borrowing permitted, but this is taken as a given, predetermined amount. In the model to be presented below, the amount to be borrowed is admitted explicit as a decision variable.

[2] An examination of the role of physical capital in the production function is made by V. L. Smith in *Investment and Production*, Harvard University Press, Cambridge, Mass., 1961. This study indicates that the presence of capital alters the role of the production constraint when comparing decisions concerning long-term vs. short-term inputs, and is devoted to integrating the theory of production and the theory of capital.

is: What is the optimum rate of output, given demand, cost, and market structure? Consequently, a flow approach and the formulation there employed is best suited to obtain the answer desired. By redirecting our attention to the firm's desired stock of capital, and thus changing the underlying problem to which the implications of the model are of interest, an alternative view of the firm becomes pertinent.

This chapter is separated into two major parts. Part A presents the model with both an analytical and graphic solution. Its relations to and implications for several other areas of economic theory are briefly discussed in footnotes. In Part B the investment equation is derived, and the implied aggregative relation, in which we are primarily interested, is obtained. A short summary section concludes the chapter.

A. A Theory of the Firm

This part is composed of six sections. The first section presents the basic setting of the model and defines the various quantities used in the development. Section 2 is devoted to examining the characteristics of the two functions governing the dollar rate of return on the firm's stocks of assets and liabilities. Thus prepared, the properties of the components of the profits function, net revenues, and debt costs are investigated in section 3. Having structured the model, the optimizing conditions are obtained analytically in the fourth section. These conditions are found diagrammatically in section 5, in which an alternative set of mutually consistent assumptions is invoked, thereby allowing the theoretical positions used in the development to be understood more thoroughly. The sixth and concluding section discusses the importance of the wealth constraint.

A1. The Setting and Definitions. Consider a firm at a given point in time as holding a portfolio consisting of stocks of assets, a, and liabilities, l.[3] These stocks will be measured in "standard units," or in

---

[3] Actually, the firm has a portfolio consisting of several distinct assets and liabilities. We will assume that the firm is able to uniquely identify the source of all earnings and expenditures, and that the earnings (payments) which result from interactions between assets (liabilities) can be allocated to the individual assets (liabilities) such that no explicit introduction of yields which are the result of these interactions need be introduced. We may then proceed as if all assets and liabilities may be considered as homogeneous units, thus allowing us to refer unambiguously to a and l, thereby simplifying the presentation of the model. Also, by ignoring interactions, we may consider the results obtained for homogeneous a as holding for all its components, in particular physical capital, and thereby use the model to derive an expression for the desired stock of capital.

real terms (which may be thought of as constant dollars).[4] The firm will be considered as a unit which acquires and sells assets in the asset market, issues and redeems liabilities in the capital market, and uses the assets so obtained to produce units of output. It sells the output so produced in the product market. Thus, the entrepreneur deals in three distinct markets: the product market, the capital market, and the asset market.

So that undivided attention might be focused on the key concepts and mechanisms at work in this model, and to maintain as much simplicity in the presentation as possible, it has been decided to ignore for the moment interactions and complexities which accompany the introduction of dynamic changes, and to present the firm as making its decisions in a static framework.

This decision has several implications. *First*, at the moment a decision is made, the situation is intended by the decision maker to have been altered for all time. We are, thus, concerned primarily with long-run phenomena. Underlying conditions may change, necessitating new decisions, but the firm is directed toward reaching an equilibrium position dictated by the new conditions. *Second*, because of the resulting "changeless" nature of a decision, a liability unit may be regarded as a consol, and its attached coupon a perpetuity. Other important implications of this treatment of time will be noted below.

The prices at which transactions occur for assets and liabilities in the capital market will be denoted as P_a and P_l, respectively. Since yields are expected to be constant and perpetual streams, the true yields (ρ_a and ρ_l) are related to the prices by the nominal yields (r_a and r_l) through the following fundamental equations:

$$(1) \qquad\qquad P_l = \frac{r_l}{\rho_l}$$

and

$$(2) \qquad\qquad P_a = \frac{r_a}{\rho_a},$$

---

[4] The problem of ignoring quality changes by measuring the same class of asset (e.g., physical capital) at different points in time with a "constant dollar unit" will not concern us here, although it will below when appropriate definitions of the relevant variables are needed for the purposes of testing the propositions obtained.

where the dimensions of the terms in the equations are

$$\text{Price } (P) = \$/\text{unit},$$

$$\text{Nominal yield } (r) = \frac{\$/\text{unit}}{\text{time}},$$

$$\text{True yield } (\rho) = \frac{\$/\$}{\text{time}}.[5]$$

These equations indicate that, when dealing with perpetuities, price is equal to the capitalized value (at the true rate) of the income stream generated by the unit.

The wealth of the firm (W) is defined as the difference between the market value of its assets and liabilities:

$$(3) \qquad W = P_a a - P_l l.$$

Wealth may thus be regarded as the net worth of the firm. Because of the decision above to eliminate changes over time, wealth is taken as a given, fixed constant at the time decisions to alter the portfolio are made. Thus, equity financing, which would change wealth, is eliminated from consideration. If an expansion of the asset side of the portfolio is desired, the sole source of financing admitted must come as a result of corresponding expansion of the firm's liabilities.

With these basic considerations in mind, the following definitions are made:

Q: quantity of output produced and sold in the product market. For any long-run output level, Q, there is an optimal value of a, the stock of assets, which is determined by the long-run average cost function. Assume that a one-to-one correspondence exists between the level of output, Q, and the associated stock of assets, a. The inverse of this relationship defines the long-run production function:

$$(4) \qquad Q = Q(a).$$

P_d: unit price of output sold in the product market. The *demand curve* in the product market is defined as

$$(5) \qquad P_d = P_d(Q).$$

---

[5] Thus, r_l may be regarded as the coupon rate on a bond while ρ_l is the true yield to the holder, or the rate of interest.

Note that this is both the current and long-run demand curve since we are assuming a static environment.

C_q: total costs per period incurred in producing the output of the firm. This will be considered as consisting of two separable components, C_c and C, below.

C_c: total costs incurred in producing the units made and sold during the period, exclusive of interest payments on the firm's outstanding liabilities. The level of these costs is a function of output,

(6) $$C_c = C_c(Q).$$

C: debt costs represented by the payments on the firm's liabilities,

(7) $$C = r_l l.$$

Total costs are defined, then, as

(8) $$C_q = C_c(Q) + C.$$

R_q: total gross revenues obtained by selling the period's output in the product market,

(9) $$R_q = P_d(Q)Q.$$

R: total net revenues, or gross revenues net of costs of production. It is thus implied that

(10) $$R = R_q - C_c \equiv r_a a.$$

π: profits per period, or

(11) $$\pi = R - C \equiv r_a a - r_l l.$$

A2. The Gross Return Functions

A2.a. The Gross Return on Assets, r_a. The nominal yield on assets, r_a (i.e., the rate of profit on assets gross of interest costs on debt), depends on the demand curve in the product market [equation (5)], the level of production costs, and the production function relating output to units of assets [equation (4)]. From equation (10), r_a may be written

$$(12) \qquad r_a = \frac{R_q - C_c}{a}.$$

By substitution of (4) into (9) and (6) and then these into (12), r_a is found to be a function of the quantity of assets only:

$$(13) \qquad r_a = \frac{P_d[Q(a)]Q(a) - C_c[Q(a)]}{a} = g(a).$$

Assume that the production function is such that there are constant returns to scale (i.e., the long-run average cost function, exclusive of debt costs, is horizontal).[6] This implies that in the long run, total production costs exclusive of interest payments will be proportional to output:

$$(14) \qquad C_c(Q) = k_1 Q \quad (k_1 = \text{constant}).$$

Assume further that an additional characteristic of the production function is that for any long-run rate of output, the optimal stock of assets is proportional to that output:

$$(15) \qquad Q(a) = k_2 a \quad (k_2 = \text{constant}).$$

Then it follows that in the long run the shape of the g function can be shown to depend solely on the demand curve for the firm's output which obtains in the product market. By substituting (14) and (15) into (13) we find

$$(16) \qquad r_a = \frac{P_d(k_2 a)k_2 a - k_1 k_2 a}{a} = k_2 P_d(k_2 a) - k_1 k_2.$$

---

[6] There are long precedents in the literature which argue for acceptability of these assumptions, especially in the long run. Cf., e.g., R. M. Solow, "A Contribution to the Theory of Economic Growth," *Quarterly Journal of Economics*, 1956, pp. 65–94; "Technical Change and the Aggregate Production Function," *Review of Economics and Statistics*, 1957, pp. 312–320, etc.; K. J. Arrow, *et al.*, "Capital-Labor Substitution and Economic Efficiency," *Review of Economics and Statistics*, 1961, pp. 225–251; and B. S. Minhas, "The Homohypallagic Production Function, Factory-Intensity Reversals, and the Heckscher-Ohlin Theorem," *Journal of Political Economy*, 1962, pp. 138–162. Constant unit costs of production are cogently argued for in, e.g., P. W. S. Andrews, *Manufacturing Business*, The Macmillan Company, London, 1949; J. S. Bain, *Barriers to New Competition, Their Character and Consequences in Manufacturing Industries*, Harvard University Press, Cambridge, Mass., 1956; and alternative theories discussed by H. R. Edwards, "Price Formation in Manufacturing Industry and Excess Capacity," *Oxford Economic Papers*, 1955, pp. 94–118.

Thus, differentiating with respect to a,

(17) $$r'_a = k_2 \frac{dP_d}{dQ} \frac{dQ}{da} = k_2^2 \frac{dP_d}{dQ} \leq 0$$

and

(18) $$r''_a = k_2^2 \frac{d^2P_d}{dQ^2} \frac{dQ}{da} = k_2^3 \frac{d^2P_d}{dQ^2} ,$$

where the inequality in (17) reflects the competitive conditions which may prevail in the product market. In the limiting case of perfect product markets, the equality holds and the r_a curve, like the demand curve, is a horizontal straight line.

A2.b. The Rate of Payments on Liabilities, r_l. The nominal yield the firm must pay on its liabilities (i.e., the average coupon rate on its bonds), depends, for a given ρ_l, on the price at which the bond is issued [from equation (1)]. Assume that the firm follows a policy of issuing all its bonds (i.e., its liabilities) at a constant price, which we may denote as the par value, P_l. We will then assume that the coupon rate will be an increasing function of the ratio between the value of the firm's liabilities and its wealth (its debt/equity ratio):[7]

(19) $$r_l = f\left(\frac{P_l l}{W}\right).$$

Wealth, as noted above, is taken as fixed for the purposes of the model. Thus, the r_l curve may be written as a function of l alone, and the shape of the curve is described by the following two relations:

(20) $$r'_l > 0,$$

(21) $$r''_l \geq 0.$$

where the double conditions on (21) merely indicate a lack of precise knowledge concerning the form of the f function.[8]

Having thus determined the salient characteristics of the functions which determine the dollar return on assets and liabilities, we now examine the properties of the total net revenues and debt costs functions.

---

[7] This assumption is that made by, among many others, F. and V. Lutz in their classic work, *The Theory of Investment of the Firm*, Princeton University Press, Princeton, N.J. 1951, and Modigliani and Miller, cf. footnote 18, below.

[8] This ambiguity will be resolved in Part B, below.

A3. *The Net Revenues and Debt Costs Functions*

A3.a. Total Net Revenues (R). The total net revenues function [equation (10)] has slope and curvature as follows:

$$(22) \qquad R' \equiv \frac{dR}{da} = r_a + ar'_2,$$

$$(23) \qquad R'' \equiv \frac{d^2R}{da^2} = 2r'_a + ar''_a,$$

where R' will be defined as marginal net revenues. Invoking the same assumptions as in the derivation of equation (16) (i.e., constant current unit costs and a production function with constant returns to scale), and substituting for r_a in (22) and (23) the expression in (16), we obtain

$$(24) \qquad R' = k_2 P_d(Q) - k_1 k_2 + ak_2^2 \frac{dP_d}{dQ},$$

$$(25) \qquad R'' = k_2^2 \left(2 \frac{dP_d}{dQ} + ak_2 \frac{d^2 P_d}{dQ^2} \right).$$

Again the dependence on the demand curve in the product market is evident.

Perfect product market. In this case, as in the previous section, both dP_d/dQ and d^2P_d/dQ^2 are zero and $P_d(Q)$ is a constant $(= P_d)$ so that expressions (24) and (25) become

$$(26) \qquad R' = k_2(P_d - k_1),$$

$$(27) \qquad R'' = 0.$$

Thus, as long as the market price is greater than the current costs of production per unit, marginal net revenues will be positive and the R function will be linear increasing, as indicated in Fig. 1(a). This proposition is consistent with conclusions derived from the conventional theory of the firm formulated in terms of flow variables. If current costs of production per unit are greater than the market price of the product, then even in the short run the firm should produce nothing, or else earn negative profits, i.e., incur losses.

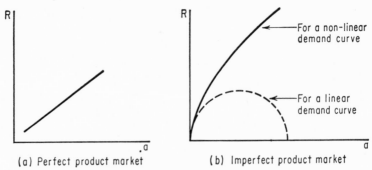

Fig. 1. The relation between total net revenues (R) and the quantity of assets (a), assuming constant unit costs of production and constant returns to scale

Imperfect product market. If the product market is imperfect, the demand curve is nonhorizontal and equations (24) and (25) are unaltered. The signs of these two expressions are ambiguous. Nonetheless, since marginal net revenues may be expected to decrease as more units are produced, we will assume R'' to be negative. In fact, if the demand curve is linear the sign of (25) is unambiguously negative[9] and the net revenues curve will be as given in the dotted line in Fig. 1(b).

A3.b. Total Debt Costs (C). The total debt costs function [equation (7)] is a function of l alone.[10] Thus, the properties of the C function are as follows:

$$(28) \qquad\qquad C' \equiv \frac{dC}{dl} = r_l + lr'_l > 0,$$

$$(29) \qquad\qquad C'' \equiv \frac{d^2C}{dl^2} = 2r'_l + lr''_l > 0.$$

The positive signs of these derivatives are implied by equations (20) and (21).

Having inquired into the characteristics of the component elements of the profits relation, we can now examine the conditions under which an entrepreneur's asset-liability portfolio will be optimal.

---

[9] That is, $d^2P_d/dQ^2 = 0$.

[10] This is because the r_l curve is itself dependent solely on l, given P_l and W; see section A2.b, above.

A4. The Maximization Conditions. The goal of the firm is to arrange its portfolio of assets and liabilities so that the utility of the owners will be maximized. Utility will be taken as a monotonically increasing function of profits, thus allowing us to deal directly with the profits function. Formally, this may be written as

$$(30) \qquad \text{Max } U = \pi^{-1}(U) = r_a a - r_l l$$

subject to

$$(31) \qquad P_a a - P_l l \leq W = P_a a_0 - P_l l_0,$$

where a_0 and l_0 are the initial values of the firm's (real) stocks.

There are two points to be noted. First, since the firm can always increase its profits by increasing its stock of assets while not increasing its liabilities, it will pay the firm never to allow any "slack" to develop in the wealth constraint. Thus, the inequality in the constraint of (31) may be replaced by an equality.[11]

Second, before turning to the implications of the model, we must be clear as to what is variable and what is constant. In the maximization procedure, a and l are decision variables and, as such, with given prices, can clearly be varied by the entrepreneur at his discretion. The variables P_i and r_i ($i = a, l$) are related through ρ_i by equations (1) and (2). We may choose to define any one of these three variables as constant for the firm, and let changes induced by alterations in the asset-liability portfolio be reflected in the other two. Accordingly, in developing the argument below, we will regard P_a and P_l as fixed. This implies, then, that the firm can acquire assets at a fixed price with the variable yield, and that it can issue debt at some constant par value.

The optimality conditions can be obtained from (30) and (31) by rewriting the problem in terms of the Lagrange multiplier, λ,

$$(32) \qquad \text{Max } L = r_a a - r_l l + \lambda [P_a(a_0 - a) - P_l(l_0 - l)],$$

---

[11] This implies that $r_a > 0$ when a is optimal. Although, for some a, r_a may be negative, the firm will not operate at this point as long as there exists some opportunity where it can loan and receive a positive return. This may require $l < 0$, i.e., the firm becomes a lender (e.g., it invests in government securities, or acquires shares in other corporations). However, the central point remains unaltered—that in the relevant range no slack will exist in the wealth constraint when the firm is at equilibrium.

from which the (first-order) equilibrium conditions are found to be

$$(33) \qquad \frac{\partial L}{\partial a} = r_a + ar_a' - \lambda P_a = 0,$$

$$(34) \qquad \frac{\partial L}{\partial l} = r_l + lr_l' - \lambda P_l = 0,$$

$$(35) \qquad \frac{\partial L}{\partial \lambda} = P_a(a_0 - a) - P_l(l_0 - l) = 0.$$

The first two of these conditions may be combined and written as

$$(36) \qquad \lambda = \frac{r_a + ar_a'}{P_a} = \frac{r_l + lr_l'}{P_l}.$$

The value of λ in these conditions is the marginal rate of profit which will accrue to the firm with respect to a unit change in wealth[12] (dimension: \$/\$/time or 1/time). This can be easily shown. Taking the total differentials of the profit equation (11) and the wealth equation (3), we obtain

$$(37) \qquad d\pi = (r_a + ar_a') \, da - (r_l + lr_l') \, dl,$$

$$(38) \qquad dW = P_a \, da - P_l \, dl.$$

Substituting (36) into (37),

$$(39) \qquad d\pi = \lambda(P_a \, da - P_l \, dl).$$

Finally, substituting (38) into (39) and rearranging terms yields the desired result,

$$(40) \qquad \lambda = \frac{d\pi}{dW}.$$

Thus, at equilibrium the firm will adjust its asset-liability portfolio so that marginal net revenues and marginal debt costs are propor-

---

[12] That is, the marginal rate of return accruing to the firm from an increase in its net worth.

tional to the price of assets and liabilities, respectively, where the common factor of proportionality is the marginal return on wealth.[13]

A5. Diagrammatic Exposition. The maximizing conditions can also be obtained diagrammatically, as is done in Fig. 2. This approach requires a change in perspective, which is helpful as it allows us an alternative means by which to view the problem. In the analytic development of the preceding section, we held prices constant and allowed changes in a and l to be reflected by compensating changes in the true and nominal yields (ρ_i and r_i, respectively). Since shifts in the portfolio result in corresponding changes in nominal yields, on which profits depend, this approach was applicable.

Diagrammatically, however, we proceed by examining budget lines and iso-profit curves. Once a portfolio is specified, the nominal yields are fixed constants for each level of profits. Thus, we will now view each point on a given iso-profit curve as corresponding to a fixed couplet of nominal yields (r_a, r_l) and regard movements along an iso-profit curve as reflecting compensating changes in true yields and prices. Hence, prices replace nominal yields as the variable quantity. This will allow us to examine the effects on desired portfolios caused by changes in the transactions ratio between assets and liabilities. The final results are, of course, identical.

The curves in Fig. 2 are iso-profit curves ($\pi_0 < \pi_1 < \pi_2 < \ldots$). The shape of these curves may be deduced from the relationship between marginal net revenues (R') and marginal debt costs (C') on the one hand and that between R and a and C and l on the other. The budget (wealth) constraint may then be added and the equilibrium

---

[13] An obvious analogy to the rudimentary theory of consumer choice can be seen here (cf., *inter alia*, J. L. Mosak, *General-Equilibrium Theory in International Trade*, Principia Press, Bloomington, Indiana, 1944, chap. 1). The optimality conditions (36) are similar to those of the theory of exchange. There, the optimality conditions indicate that another unit of a commodity should be acquired until the marginal utility which it provides is proportional to its market price. The factor of proportionality is the marginal utility of income, where income is defined as the value, at given market prices, of the initial commodity bundle (his supply) possessed by the consumer (Mosak, p. 10). The similarity should, of course, come as no surprise in that this definition of income is directly analogous to our definition of wealth. In fact, since these quantities are the market values of the real *stocks* owned at the beginning of the period in question, it appears that our use of the term "wealth" is better chosen than the term "income" in exchange theory. Of course, in expanded, more sophisticated treatments of general- equilibrium theory, income is introduced as a true flow.

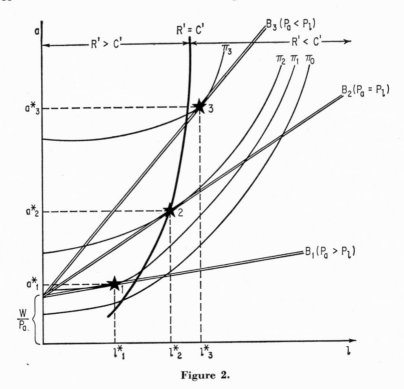

Figure 2.

conditions obtained where the budget line touches the highest iso-profit curve. At this point the optimum portfolio (a^*, l^*) will be given.

A5.a. The Iso-profit Lines. To determine the slope of an iso-profit curve in the a, l plane, we must find da/dl when $d\pi = 0$. Setting equation (37) to zero and solving for da/dl, we find that

$$(41) \qquad \frac{da}{dl} = \frac{C'}{R'},$$

from which the following relationship between the slope and marginal net revenues and costs is discovered:

$$(42) \qquad \text{slope} \begin{Bmatrix} < 1 \\ = 1 \\ > 1 \end{Bmatrix} \text{ if } \begin{Bmatrix} R' > C' \\ R' = C' \\ R' < C' \end{Bmatrix}.$$

It is instructive to work through the economic interpretation of these conditions. In order to keep profits constant (and, thus, to stay on the same iso-profit curve) while shifting portfolios, revenues and costs[14] must change by equal amounts and in the same direction. As long as $R' > C'$, each unit of asset that is added to the portfolio adds more in revenue than in costs, corresponding to the increase of one unit in liabilities. Thus, as long as $R' > C'$, more than one unit of l must be added for every unit of assets added, in order that profits remain constant. The slope, then, of an iso-profit curve in Fig. 2 will be less than unity when $R' > C'$.

Similarly, if $R' = C'$, one unit added to both assets and liabilities will change costs and revenues equally so that profits remain constant and the slope of the iso-profit curve is, in this case, equal to unity. When $R < C'$ the argument is directly analogous to the case in which $R' > C'$ but the inequalities are all reversed, with the result that the slope is greater than unity.

Given this relation between the marginal quantities and the slope of an iso-profit curve as summarized in (42), for what combinations of asset units and liability units are marginal revenues likely to be greater than, equal to, and less than marginal costs?

When a is large, relative to l, marginal costs may be expected to be quite low. This is so since r_l is an increasing function of the debt/equity ratio, as indicated in (19). We would expect $R' > C'$ for portfolios of this sort. With a given number of asset units, as the number of liability units is increased, marginal costs increase, eventually becoming equal to R' and, finally, greater than R'.[15]

Thus, as drawn in Fig. 2, the iso-profit lines curve upward to the right and, since higher profits will be obtained as a increases when l is constant, higher iso-profit lines are found by moving upward on the diagram.

A5.b. The Budget (Wealth) Constraint. Rewriting the wealth constraint of (31) so that it might be easily introduced into the a, l plane of Fig. 2, we obtain

$$(43) \qquad a = \frac{W}{P_a} + \frac{P_l}{P_a} l.$$

---

[14] Throughout this section the term "revenues" will refer to total net revenues (R) and "costs" to total debt costs (C). The same convention will be followed with respect to the corresponding marginal quantities.

[15] From equations (28) and (29) debt costs are seen to increase at an increasing rate, thus leading to this conclusion.

The first term is the intercept shown in Fig. 2. The second indicates that the slope of the budget line is the ratio between the price at which the firm sells liabilities and acquires assets in the capital market.[16]

Three budget constraints, corresponding to three different values of the slope (P_l/P_a), are drawn in Fig. 2 (i.e., B_1, B_2, and B_3). All have been given the same intercept, such that the changing slope may be regarded as the result of changing the price of liabilities while the price of assets remains constant.

The three cases will also be useful in analyzing the resultant change in the equilibrium condition due to a change in the price of bonds. They will be analyzed in turn:

Case I: $P_l/P_a < 1$, Budget Line B_1

Rewriting the optimality conditions of (36), we obtain

$$(44) \qquad\qquad R' = C' \frac{P_a}{P_l}.$$

When $P_a > P_l$, condition (44) is satisfied only if $R' > C'$, as we saw above. Thus, in Fig. 2, the optimality conditions for this case are fulfilled at ★1, and an optimal portfolio of a_1^* and l_1^* is indicated. The rate of profit earned by the firm at this point is π_1.

Case II: $P_l/P_a = 1$, Budget Line B_2

In this instance, $P_a = P_l$ and the condition of (44) indicates that the optimal portfolio is reached when $R' = C'$. This portfolio is denoted as a_2^* and l_2^* in Fig. 2, and the point of tangency is marked by ★2 at profit level π_2.

Comparing the equilibrium states of Cases I and II, it is evident that profits have increased as the firm has grown (i.e., $\pi_2 > \pi_1$, $a_2^* > a_1^*$), and the growth which occurs in II relative to I is due to the change in P_l relative to P_a. This conclusion, of course, rests on the previously made attendant assumptions and is discussed in more detail in section A6.

Case III: $P_l/P_a > 1$, Budget Line B_3

The condition of (44) will now hold only if $R' < C'$, which means that the firm can obtain more than one unit of assets of every extra unit of liabilities it incurs (e.g., prices have changed such that the price at which a bond of a given coupon is issued is now higher relative to the

---

[16] As noted above, the prices are no longer fixed constants.

price of machines than formerly). Thus, borrowing rates have fallen. Even though it must pay an ever increasing rate on each unit of liability it adds, its total profit will increase since, by taking on more assets than liabilities, its total net revenues increase more than total debt costs, up to the point at which (44) is fulfilled. These conditions are satisfied at point ★3, with balance sheet defined by a_3^*, l_3^* and profits of π_3 in Fig. 2.

A6. The Effect of the Wealth Constraint. We find, then, that with a given wealth, the optimal size[17] of the firm increases as the price of liability units increases relative to the price of asset units. This, of course, is what we should expect. As the price at which the firm can take on an extra unit of liability increases (e.g., as the price of bonds increases), the firm can acquire more real assets (P_a constant, say) for a given increase in real liabilities. Thus, the firm will be larger under these circumstances.[18]

Yet, for any given ratio of P_l to P_a, the optimal size of the firm is finite. This is true because debt costs are increasing faster than net revenues after a certain point (i.e., $C'' > 0$ while $R'' < 0$). The crucial assumption in our solution is that interest costs tend to rise with an increasing debt-equity ratio [equation (20)], and this assumption appears perfectly acceptable.[19]

It is interesting to note that a previous argument advanced by Kalecki[20] also basically depends on wealth as the ultimate delimiter of a firm's size. His position can be summarized as in Fig. 3.

---

[17] As discussed by N. R. Collins and L. E. Preston, in their article "The Size Structure of the Largest Industrial Firms, 1909–1958," *American Economic Review*, 1961, pp. 986–1003, the best measure of firm size has been widely debated. Assets are probably as good a measure of size as any, and since they (1) have been used by many previous writers concerned with the problem and (2) are immediately available from the formulation of our model, assets are used as our measure here.

[18] With r_l constant, the effect of increasing P_l is to reduce the firm's true cost of capital, P_l, as is indicated in equation (1). Expansion is thereby encouraged.

[19] Thus, for example, even F. Modigliani and M. Miller, who, in their article "The Cost of Capital, Corporation Finance and the Theory of Investment," *American Economic Review*, 1958, pp. 261–297, tend to depart from many of the received doctrines in the field of finance, argue that "Economic theory and market experience both suggest that the yields demanded by lenders tend to increase with the debt-equity ratio of the borrowing firm (or individual)" (p. 273). See also their "Reply," *American Economic Review*, 1950, pp. 665–669, and "Dividend Policy, Growth and the Valuation of Shares," *Journal of Business*, 1961, pp. 411–433.

[20] M. Kalecki, "The Principle of Increasing Risk," *Economica*, 1937, pp. 440–447. The principle is utilized by L. R. Klein in deriving the investment equation in *Economic Fluctuations in the United States, 1921–1941*, John Wiley & Sons, Inc., New York, 1950.

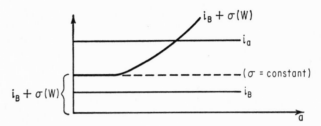

Fig. 3. Kalecki's "principle of increasing risk" and optimal size of firm

In Fig. 3, i_a is the marginal yield on assets (which Kalecki argues will be constant with no large-scale uneconomies and perfect markets), i_B is the cost of funds, and σ is an internally computed risk factor. As long as i_a is greater than $i_B + \sigma$, increases in the stock of assets will be desired. In particular, if i_B and σ were always constant (dashed line), infinite increases will be desired. Kalecki's point, however, is that σ is not a constant (even apart from a probable upward-sloping i_B curve), but increases as the firm's "own capital" (i.e., its wealth) shrinks in proportion to the increased borrowing made necessary by the expansion of assets.[21] Thus, in σ the wealth constraint is exerted.[22]

B. The Investment Equation

In Part A we have presented a model of the firm which emphasizes the firm's stock positions and, in addition, derived the equilibrium con-

---

[21] Thus, Kalecki writes: "The smaller is the own capital of an entrepreneur investing the (given) amount . . . the greater risk he incurs. For his possible losses bear a greater proportion to his wealth and—since the amount of credits considered by his creditors as "normal" is in a certain proportion to his own capital—the danger of 'illiquidity' is greater too."

[22] The force of the "Principle of Increasing Risk" was diminished somewhat by S. Wellisz ("Entrepreneur's Risk, Lender's Risk, and Investment," *Review of Economic Studies*, 1952–53, pp. 105–114), who showed that "although the entrepreneur's risk and the lender's risk increase with the size of the loan, given an arbitrary amount of the entrepreneur's own capital, the risk of the enterprise as a whole declines with increasing size." Wellisz concludes that, owing to the conflicting directions assumed by these different risk functions, the net effect is ambiguous. Nonetheless, it is the entrepreneur who must make the decisions to attempt expansion. Since his personal risk increases with the larger loans which are needed for expansion, it is to be expected that his decisions will reflect this fact and Kalecki's conclusion will hold.

ditions toward which the firm will strive. In this part we will use this model to develop an investment equation. We will find that this equation is fully testable, and, as such, we may consider tests of this relation as comprising a set of checks on the validity of the model as a whole. Chapter 4 reports on the results of the battery of tests to which the investment equation derived here was subjected.

This part is divided into four sections. In section 1, the optimal stock of assets is obtained from the conditions of equilibrium given by the model. Utilizing the heuristic that in any given finite period (a year, say) actual investment will be proportional to the difference between actual and desired stocks,[23] we obtain the investment equation in section 2. Since this investment relation was derived from a model of one representative firm, while we are interested in the aggregated gross physical investment of the private business sector of the economy, it is necessary to modify our results in such a way that aggregative tests may be made. The aggregation procedures used for this purpose are discussed in the third section.[24] Part B concludes with a brief discussion of the possible importance of decisions made in or implied by the supply side of the capital goods market.

B1. The Desired Stock of Capital.

From the equilibrium-conditions equations (33), (34), and (35), it is possible to obtain the desired stock of assets at the beginning of the period. Rewriting these conditions in matrix form, we obtain

$$(45) \qquad (a, l, \lambda) \begin{bmatrix} r'_a & 0 & P_a \\ 0 & r'_l & -P_l \\ -P_a & -P_l & 0 \end{bmatrix} = (-r_a, -r_l, W).$$

---

[23] Of course, when discussing those kinds of assets for which transaction times are very short (e.g., money), this factor of proportionality may become unity, even in periods as short as a day. But in the case of real capital, the time delays incurred in the planning and construction periods may be substantial. Thus, it is expected that only a fraction of desired investment will be completed in a period of a year's duration.

[24] It should, of course, be noted that another important argument for careful identification of assumptions at the micro level, such as that in Part A above, is that this type of development readily allows us to inspect the modifications introduced by aggregation.

Solving for a,[25]

$$(46) \qquad a^* = \frac{P_a r_l' W + P_l^2 r_a - P_l P_a r_l}{P_a^2 r_l' - P_l^2 r_a'}.$$

To simplify, we may choose our units of measurement such that $P_a = P_l = P$, a constant under the assumptions used in the derivation of the equilibrium conditions. Substituting for r_a and r_l through equations (1) and (2), we obtain[26]

$$(47) \qquad a^* = \alpha_1 \frac{W}{P} + \beta_1 (\rho_a - \rho_l),$$

where[27]

$$(48) \qquad \beta_1 = (\rho_l' - \rho_a')^{-1}, \qquad \alpha_1 = \beta_1 \rho_l'.$$

Note that a^*, the desired stock of real assets, is an increasing function of real wealth[28] and ρ_a, and a decreasing function of ρ_l.[29] For the purposes

---

[25] Rewrite the equilibrium conditions (33)–(35):

(a) $\qquad\qquad\qquad\qquad a r_a' - \lambda P_a = -r_a,$

(b) $\qquad\qquad\qquad\qquad -r_l' l + \lambda P_l = r_l,$

(c) $\qquad\qquad\qquad\qquad -a P_a + l P_l = -W.$

Substitute into (a) the expressions for λ and l obtained from (b) and (c), respectively:

(d) $\qquad a r_a' - \dfrac{P_a}{P_l} r_l - \left(\dfrac{P_a}{P_l}\right)^2 a r_l' + \dfrac{P_a}{P_l} r_l' \dfrac{W}{P_l} = -r_a.$

Rearrange terms such that those containing a are on the left:

(e) $\qquad a\left[r_a' - \left(\dfrac{P_a}{P_l}\right)^2 r_l' \right] = a\left[\dfrac{P_l^2 r_a' - P_a^2 r_l'}{P_l^2} \right]$

$$\qquad\qquad\qquad\qquad = \frac{P_a}{P_l} r_l - \frac{P_a W r_l'}{P_l^2} - r_a.$$

Equation (46) is obtained by dividing (e) by the expression in the squared brackets.

[26] In this substitution, the assumption of constant P implies $P_a' = P_l' = 0$.

[27] The effect of the presence of the "residual" P in the denominator of the first term is to reduce all three terms in the expression to a common dimension: units. The dimension of β_1 is time/$/units^2 and α_1 is a pure number.

[28] The dimensions of W and P are $ and $/unit, respectively. Thus, W/P is measured in units, i.e., in real terms.

[29] Since $\rho_l' > 0$ and $\rho_a' \leq 0$, both α_1 and β_1 are positive.

of empirical investigation we will assume that α_1 and β_1 are constant. The economic implication of this assumption is that we are now employing linear approximations for the nominal yield curves on both liabilities and assets [equations (19) and (13), respectively].[30] The effect of this assumption is that the desired real stock is then a linear function of real wealth and the difference between the expected long-run average rate of return on assets and the interest rate.

It was noted[31] at the outset of Part A that, by our assumptions, the above results may be taken to hold for a given asset, e.g., physical

---

[30]
$$\alpha_1 = \rho_l'(\rho_l' - \rho_a')^{-1} = c_1 = \text{constant},$$

$$\beta_1 = (\rho_l' - \rho_a')^{-1} = c_2 = \text{constant},$$

$$\therefore \quad \rho_l' = \frac{c_1}{c_2} = \text{constant} = c_3, \text{ say}.$$

Integrating,

(x) $$\rho_l = c_3 l + c_4.$$

Economically, we must assume that

$$c_3, c_4 > 0.$$

From equation (1) and the assumption of constant price,

$$\frac{dP_l}{dl} = \frac{\rho_l r_l' - r_l \rho_l'}{\rho_l^2} = 0$$

or

$$\rho_l r_l' = r_l \rho_l'.$$

Substituting from (x),

(y) $$(c_3 l + c_4) r_l' = c_3 r_l,$$

from which

$$r_l' = c_3 r_l / (c_3 l + c_4) > 0,$$

consistent with equation (20). However, differentiating r_l' with respect to l,

$$r_l'' = \frac{c_3^2 r_l - c_3^2 r_l}{(c_3 l + c_4)^2} = 0,$$

which implies that a linear function ($r_l = c_5 l + c_6$) is a solution to (y).

Analogously, the assumption that ρ_a' is constant can be shown to imply that r_a is a linear function of a, indicating that a linear approximation to the curve described in equation (13) is implied by the assumption of constant coefficients.

[31] Cf. footnote 3, above.

capital.[32] Thus, the desired stock of capital at the beginning of the period (K_t^D) may be denoted

(49) $$K_t^D = \alpha' W_t + \beta'(\rho_K - r)_t.$$

The subscript on wealth indicates the existing amount at the beginning of period t. Both W and K^D are in real terms (constant dollars), ρ_K is the expected long-run return on capital, r is the true (not nominal) rate of interest, and the coefficients of (49) are related to those of (47) by (50):

(50) $$\alpha' = \frac{\alpha_1}{P}, \qquad \beta' = \beta_1.$$

B2. The Investment Equation. For some assets, in particular those with low transactions costs (e.g., money and some securities), the length of time it takes to adjust actual stocks to desired levels is short, relative to the period for which we observe changes in the variables themselves. Thus, we may interpret the observed quantities as the corresponding desired amounts.[33] However, for assets with high transactions costs (and/or construction lags), the period of adjustments is much longer. It is this property which characterizes the asset in which we are interested, capital goods (K).

Investment is viewed here as the process which equates the actual stock of capital to the desired stock. This procedure implies frequent or continued disequilibrium. In particular, investment (or disinvestment) is undertaken in an attempt to approach the equilibrium (desired) position if the yield on capital is not equal to that on other assets when the portfolio is reviewed.

Thus, if K_t^D is given by (49), K_t is the existing stock of plant and equipment at the end of period $t - 1$ (i.e., the beginning of t), and D_t is the deterioration which is expected to occur to the capital stock during

---

[32] Also, since we will expect the magnitude of noncapital assets held by the firm to be closely related to the capital stock (especially over the long run), this one particular asset appears more likely than others to be consistent with the spirit of the model.

[33] Indeed, this is the precise assumption used to great effect by A. H. Meltzer, "The Demand for Money: Evidence from the Time Series," *Journal of Political Economy*, forthcoming, and P. Cagan, "The Monetary Effects of Hyperinflation," in *Studies in the Quantity Theory of Money*, M. Friedman, ed., University of Chicago Press, Chicago, 1956; pp. 25–117.

the period, then the desired net investment in period t as of the beginning of the period (I_t^D) will be

(51) $$I_t^D = K_t^D - K_t + D_t,$$

or

(52) $$I_t^D = \alpha'W_t + \beta'(\rho_K - r)_t - K_t + D_t.$$

If, in period t, only a fraction, γ, of the desired investment is to be completed, net investment I_t in period t will be

(53) $$I_t = \gamma I_t^D.$$

Assuming further that the amount of deterioration in period t is proportional to the stock of capital at the beginning of the period (i.e., $D_t = dK_t$), net investment becomes

(54) $$I_t = \alpha W_t + \beta(\rho_K - r)_t - \gamma(1 - d)K_t,$$

where

(55) $$\alpha = \gamma\alpha', \qquad \beta = \gamma\beta'.$$

Recall that this investment equation is the result of a desired stock of capital based on long-run expected yields. Thus, temporary fluctuations in such variables as the price of machines or the operating rate at which the capital stock is expected to be employed may be among those factors which cause actual investment in any given year to depart from that expected. Accordingly, in the statistical tests of Chapter 4, the residuals of the long-term model are examined in an effort to detect the influence of these short-term factors.

B3. Aggregation Assumptions. As indicated in Chapter 1, our concern is with the aggregate expenditures of private business on plant and equipment. The model presented above was couched in the framework of a "representative firm." In this section, I present the assumptions being made in the process of aggregating so that, during interpretion of the results of the tests made in the succeeding chapter, some basis will be available for relating the quantities there obtained to those applicable to the micro relation of equation (54). The procedure to be followed relies heavily on results obtained by Theil.[34] Given the micro

---

[34] H. Theil, *Linear Aggregation of Economic Relations*, North-Holland Publishing Co., Amsterdam, 1954. The basic principles contained therein which are relevant to the present section are given by R. G. D. Allen, *Mathematical Economics*, The Macmillan Company, London, 1957, Chap. 20.

model of (54), an exact macro analogue can be obtained by assuming the macro parameters to be the arithmetic mean of their corresponding individual values and reinterpreting the measures available for the variables in our equation. Omitting time subscripts, letting γ and d be the same for all firms, and using the j subscript for the jth firm, (54) can be rewritten as

$$(56) \qquad I_j = \alpha_j W_j + \beta_j (\rho_K - r)_j + \delta K_j \quad (j = 1, 2, \ldots, n),$$

where there are n firms, $\delta = -\gamma(1 - d)$, and both α_j and β_j include γ, the speed of adjustment. Sum (56) over all firms:

$$(57) \qquad \sum_j I_j = \sum_j \alpha_j W_j + \sum_j \beta_j (\rho_K - r)_j + \delta \sum_j K_j.$$

The macro relation is of the form

$$(58) \qquad\qquad I = \alpha W + \beta (\rho_K - r) + \delta K,$$

where α and β are the macro parameters (i.e., the macro marginal propensities to invest, M.P.I., with respect to W and $(\rho_K - r)$). This approach would proceed by letting α and β in (58) represent the mean values (*unweighted*) of the corresponding micro parameters, and by interpreting our aggregate measures of W and $(\rho_K - r)$ as the weighted averages of the corresponding micro variables, where the weights are the individual M.P.I.'s (i.e., α_j and β_j).

This procedure is rejected for the present application for several reasons. First, the interpretation of the aggregate measure of W, say, as a weighted average of the individual W_j's implies that, if the α_j's had been different, another measure of W would have been obtained. But we know that the aggregate measures we have are simple sums of the individual micro quantities, and it would seem incumbent upon us to utilize a procedure which takes cognizance of this fact. Also, and perhaps more important, the measurement of α and β as the average marginal propensity of all relevant firms is not what is desired for our purposes. For explaining and forecasting aggregate investment expenditures, the parameter estimates we seek are the weighted averages of the individual marginal propensities. Thus, if the M.P.I.'s of three corner grocers are .5 and that of General Motors, say, is .1, it would be folly for the purposes of prediction to induce changes in an independent variable (e.g., a 10 per cent increase in W for all four firms) and expect changes in the total investment of these four firms corresponding to an average M.P.I. of .4. Obviously, an average M.P.I. should reflect the relative influence the activities of a given firm have on our aggregate measure of investment. Finally, the model of (58) is still not ready for statistical testing in that it is a deterministic equation.

We will use, therefore, a second approach, *viz.*, given the micro relaton of (56) and an aggregation procedure which allows us to obtain (a) a measure of W which is a simple linear sum of the W_j, and (b) a measure of $(\rho_K - r)$ which is a weighted average of the $(\rho_K - r)_j$, we must try to find a linear macro relation whose form and parameters possess the characteristics we consider desirable. Thus, we assume

$$\text{(a)} \qquad I = \sum I_j$$

$$(59) \quad \text{(b)} \qquad W = \sum W_j$$

$$\text{(c)} \qquad K = \sum K_j$$

$$\text{(d)} \qquad (\rho_K - r) = \sum_j \frac{K_j(\rho_K - r)_j}{K}.$$

The individual $(\rho_K - r)_j$'s in (d) are weighted by the proportion of total capital (K) held by the individual firm. This measure of size is deemed as good a measure of the firm's relative influence as any alternative.

The next step is to examine the relation of changes in W_j and $(\rho_K - r)_j$ to changes in W and $(\rho_K - r)$ over the time period considered. These relationships can be obtained statistically from least-squares regressions over the period:

$$\text{(a)} \qquad W_j = A_jW + B_j + u_j, \qquad j = 1, \ldots, n;$$

$$(60)$$

$$\text{(b)} \quad (\rho_K - r)_j = C_j(\rho_K - r) + D_j + v_j, \quad j = 1, \ldots, n;$$

where A_j, B_j, C_j, and D_j are the coefficients found from the regression equations, and u_j and v_j are the stochastic elements which we assume have zero means and are uncorrelated with W and $(\rho_K - r)$, respectively. Because of (59b) and (59d), we may state that

$$\sum_j A_j = \sum_j K_jC_j/K = 1$$

and

$$\sum_j B_j = \sum_j K_jD_j = 0,$$

which are obtained by summing (60) over j, having first multiplied (60b) by K_j/K.

Finally, substitution of (60), (59a), and (59c) into (57) gives

(61) $\quad I = \sum_j (A_jW + B_j + u_j)$

$$+ \sum_j \beta_j[C_j(\rho_K - r) + D_j + v_j] + \delta K,$$

which is of the form

(62) $\qquad\qquad I = \alpha W + \beta(\rho_K - r) + \delta K + \xi + u,$

where

$\qquad$ (a) $\qquad\qquad \alpha = \sum \alpha_j A_j,$

$\qquad$ (b) $\qquad\qquad \beta = \sum \beta_j C_j,$

(63) $\quad$ (c) $\qquad\qquad \delta = -\gamma(1 - d),$

$\qquad$ (d) $\qquad\qquad \xi = \sum \alpha_j B_j + \sum \beta_j D_j,$

$\qquad$ (e) $\qquad\qquad u = \sum \alpha_j u_j + \sum \beta_j v_j.$

Equation (62) is then of the same form as (58) with the addition of constant and stochastic terms.

Thus, the aggregation procedure has successfully fulfilled the criteria discussed above. *First*, the estimates of the parameters in which we are most interested (i.e., α and especially β) are the weighted averages which are desired. *Second*, the measurement of the relevant variables is exactly that for which we had hoped. In addition, a constant term, ξ, has been introduced. *Finally*, the macro equation thus obtained has required the introduction of a stochastic element, thereby making (62) immediately suitable for statistical testing.

B4. The Supply Side. Thus far, with the brief exception of the possible importance of short-term effects, discussion of the investment relation has proceeded solely in terms of the demand for capital. It is necessary to examine the extent to which the aspects of supply may be expected to affect the results presented previously.

There are two markets in which the firm must operate after deciding to undertake investment activity. *First*, there is the capital goods (physical) market, from which the firm typically purchases the equipment and plant it desires. *Second*, there is the financial market from which are obtained the funds used to make these purchases, including its own, internally generated, funds. Disruptions in either of these that curtail or hamper the flow of resources to the firm will have repercussions on the amount of investment actually undertaken, no matter what amount may otherwise be desired. Fortunately, although the model does not explicitly include these effects, consideration of the following five points leads us to substantially discount the possibility that their exclusion will materially affect the conclusions forthcoming from tests of the investment relation derived above.

First, it may be that physical supply does not pose any great problem. In at least one durable goods industry there is evidence that supply is highly elastic in the long run and "also that even over short periods of time there is a high degree of mobility of resources" in the industry.[35]

Second, supply curtailment will affect our results only when demand exceeds the industry's capacity to produce. Since output can be greatly extended beyond rated capacity over short periods of time (i.e., in periods of peak demand), we would expect those periods to be rare when this phenomenon would be important.

Third, to the extent that short-run aberrations of this sort are noticeable, they should be reflected in the residuals which result from the fitted long-term equation. These are tested for in Chapter 4.

Fourth, much evidence on business pricing policies suggests that prices may be expected to remain relatively constant even in periods of high output, and any increases that might occur are so small relative to the magnitude of the outlays and interest payments involved that for most practical purposes they may be ignored.[36]

Finally, a tightening money supply also characterizes periods of high demand and inadequate supply, and to a certain extent these conditions will be reflected in the rate of interest, already included in our model. Thus, the curtailment of physical supply may not be an important enough eventuality to seriously affect the long-run parameter estimates in the model. I will assume this is the case.

In the financial market, firms may view present conditions and decide to undertake large projects, only to find that the supply of funds is inelastic. Thus, a need for modifications in the model, or at least in the measuring procedures utilized, would be indicated.

However, periods when capital costs are relatively low (i.e., when market prices of securities are relatively high) are exactly those in which large amounts of funds are flowing into the market. The liquidity preference of the system is decreasing, and more funds are available for the

---

[35] R. Muth, "The Demand for Non-Farm Housing," pp. 29–96 in A. C. Harberger, *The Demand for Durable Goods*, University of Chicago Press, Chicago, 1960, p. 42.

[36] E.g., P. W. S. Andrews, *Manufacturing Business*, The Macmillan Company, London, 1949.

specific purpose under discussion. Also, to the extent that firms finance investment from internally generated funds, this problem is avoided. These funds must be costed (i.e., the rate of interest is still relevant), but their availability is at least partly decided upon internally (e.g., in the setting of dividend policy).

Of course, review of the results of our empirical studies will allow us to better evaluate these conjectures.

C. Concluding Remarks

In this chapter we have formulated a model of the firm which allows giving explicit attention to the stock of assets desired by the firm at any given point in time. We have derived conditions of equilibrium for this model. In particular, we found that the firm balances its asset-liability portfolio as a function of its wealth and the difference between the yield on assets and the rate of interest. Utilizing these equilibrium conditions, we obtained an expression for the desired stock of assets. This result was then used to derive an investment equation, which was aggregated in such a way that tests at the macroeconomic level could be made.

In developing this model we have carefully identified the assumptions which we have found it necessary to make. While these assumptions have seemed fairly restrictive at times, we have argued that, in the long-run context utilized, they are mostly reasonable and acceptable. Of course, the great advantage of such development lies precisely in the fact that assumptions become explicit and, as such, may be useful in profitably redirecting efforts if modifications should be desired at a later time. The acceptability of this package of assumptions may be judged better after we have reviewed the results of our empirical work in the following chapter.

CHAPTER 4

Empirical Tests and
Implications of the Model

In the preceding chapter, a model of the firm was developed from which the following investment equation was derived:

$$(1) \qquad I_t = \alpha_0 + \alpha_1 W_t + \alpha_2 (\rho_K - r)_t + \alpha_3 K_t + u_t,$$

where

I_t = aggregate gross investment expenditures by business firms on new plant and equipment during year t;

W_t = wealth (net worth) of firms at the beginning of year t;

ρ_{Kt} = the expected return on capital during year t;

r_t = the rate of interest during year t;

K_t = the aggregate capital stock of business firms at the beginning of year t; and

u_t = a stochastic error term.

In this chapter, this investment equation will be subjected to test by regression analysis. Time series data of aggregate investment expenditures by private business from 1915 through 1961, excluding the years of World War II (1941–1945), will be used.[1]

Part A discusses the techniques and data used to measure the variables in equation (1). The basic results and implications of the estimates of the coefficients are given in Part B. The model underlying equation (1) is essentially a long-run model; however, the data used to test the investment relation reflect both short- and long-term factors. Accordingly, in Part C an attempt is made to incorporate the effect of short-term considerations into the model by examining the effects of uncompleted plans of past years. The residuals of this "short-term" equation are then further studied. Part D presents comparisons of the ability of several alternative models to forecast investment expenditures of private business during the decade 1952–1961. Part E summarizes the chapter.

A. Measurement of the Variables[2]

A1. I_t: Gross Investment. The investment variable is taken as gross expenditure by private nonagricultural business on new plant and equipment. This measure differs from the official Department of Commerce definition of gross investment in that it excludes investment in inventories, investment by agricultural business, and outlays charged to current account.

It is thought that investment in inventories is related more to essentially shorter-term considerations than to those which are relevant to the present model. Thus, its inclusion would only make more difficult the task of identifying the causal elements in investment in fixed capital, which we have taken as our primary concern. Outlays charged to current

---

[1] Although various other tests of our hypothesis will also be of interest (e.g., cross sections, sector analysis, investigation of individual firms, etc.), it is thought that time series data at the aggregate level furnish an appropriate starting point. As stated by F. Modigliani and M. Zeman ("The Effect of the Availability of Funds, and the Terms Thereof, on Business Investment," pp. 263–309 in *Conference in Research and Finance*, National Bureau of Economic Research, New York, 1952): "Any theory based on simplifying assumptions cannot be expected to explain all the 'quirks' of all the individual decisions; it is only when these idiosyncrasies have been averaged out by dealing with a substantial number of cases that the influence of the basic factors upon which our theory is based can become apparent. For this reason, and because of their availability, time series data seems to be the appropriate type to use, in spite of many limitations."

[2] Detailed descriptions of the data sources and the methods of compilation used to obtain the estimates used are included in the Appendix.

account were excluded since these items are usually very short-lived assets, and it is not necessary to finance expenditures of this type with long-term capital.

Investment by agricultural business was excluded since the factors relevant to agricultural investment seem quite different from those underlying decisions in manufacturing and other trade.[3] Also, the task of measuring the yields, wealth, and capital stock variables for the agricultural sector on a basis consistent with that used for the corporate sector is exceedingly difficult. In particular, a meaningful procedure is lacking for the separation of assets of agricultural *business* from *private* assets held by individuals in the agricultural sector.

A2. W_t: Wealth. In Chapter 3, wealth was defined as the net worth of the firm. We want a measure of wealth which reflects the constraint imposed on businessmen in allocating their assets. Economic theory suggests that entrepreneurs respond to market prices and market values, at least in the long run. This implies that a relevant measure of wealth must be market oriented.[4] Therefore, we reject any measure of wealth founded on book values of net worth. Book values, of course, represent an amalgamation of many accounting conventions which, especially when aggregating across firms, may exhibit broad inconsistencies.

Accordingly, we have taken the value of the net worth of the firm to be given by the market value of its common stock. This measure of wealth may exhibit wider fluctuations over time than the concept of wealth which is relevant to the entrepreneur. Nonetheless, on the average it is a far better approximation to the measure we seek than that given by the aggregate book value of the net worth of the component firms. Measuring net worth by book values results in a mixture of varying and often conflicting methods of valuation.

A3. ρ_t: Expected Yield. The third variable which we need to measure is the expected return on real capital. We have substituted the yield on *assets* for the yield on *capital*—for two reasons. *First*, when

---

[3] For, example, the large fluctuations in output and profits which are caused by the essentially random influence of weather.

[4] These points have been made by many recent investigators who have been utilizing measures as given by market values for variables formerly measured by book values exclusively. Cf., e.g., F. Modigliani and M. Miller, *American Economic Review*, 1958, and M. J. Gordon, *The Investment, Financing and Valuation of the Corporation*, Richard D. Irwin, Inc. Homewood, Ill., 1962.

using aggregative data, it is difficult to distinguish that proportion of total profits which emanates from capital, from the proportion which accrues from holding other assets. *Second,* since capital is by far the most important component of total assets, this substitution does not make any important changes in the measure we seek. Accordingly, our notation of this variable is changed from ρ_{K_t} to ρ_t.

The expected yield is measured as the expected dollar return, $\bar{X}_t$, divided by the value of assets at the beginning of the period, V_t:

$$(2) \qquad \rho_t = \frac{\bar{X}_t}{V_t}.$$

The denominator of (2) is the market value of outstanding securities (stocks plus bonds). Thus, V_t may be interpreted as the market value of total assets less current liabilities.

We desire a measure of assets in V_t which will indicate the long-run return on investment when used in equation (1). Equity (stock) and debt (bonds) may finance some short-term investment; however, it is unlikely that short-term debt (i.e., current liabilities) will be used to finance long-term investment, the variable with which our theoretical development is concerned. Thus, V_t appears to be a more appropriate measure of the denominator we seek than either total assets or V_t plus short-term liabilities.

Given this measure of the denominator in (2), operational measurement of ρ_t is still complicated by the fact that the numerator of our definition, $\bar{X}_t$, is an *expected* dollar return and, thus, is not directly observable. The problem of measuring expected magnitudes is not a new one in economics, however. An approach similar to that used successfully by Cagan, Friedman, and others, will be used here.[5]

The behavioral assumption of this approach to measuring expectations is that expectations are revised according to experienced departures from past expected levels. Thus, if observed returns, X_t, are viewed as composed of two components—an expected, long-run component, $\bar{X}_t$, and a transitory component, X_t^T—then

$$(3) \qquad X_t = \bar{X}_t + X_t^T.$$

[5] E.g., D. Meiselman, *The Term Structure of Interest Rates,* Englewood Cliffs, N. J., Prentice-Hall, Inc., 1962; M. Nerlove, "Adaptive Expectations and Cobweb Phenomena," *Quarterly Journal of Economics,* 1958, pp. 227–240; D. E. Farrar, *The Investment Decision Under Uncertainty,* Englewood Cliffs, N. J., Prentice-Hall, Inc., 1962; P. Cagan, "The Monetary Dynamics of Hyperinflation," *op. cit.*; and M. Friedman, *A Theory of the Consumption Function, op. cit.*

The behavioral assumption may be formulated as

(4) $$\bar{X}_t - \bar{X}_{t-1} = \eta X_{t-1}^T = \eta(X_{t-1} - \bar{X}_{t-1}),$$

or[6]

(5) $$\bar{X}_t = (1 - \eta)\bar{X}_{t-1} + \eta X_{t-1}.$$

Thus, the parameter η measures the proportion of unanticipated profits realized during the past period which is expected to continue during the present period.

To allow for secular growth in $\bar{X}_t$ over the period for which our tests will be made, a growth parameter, g (which was set and held at .03, the average rate of growth in X_t during the period examined), is added to the model[7] such that the equation becomes

(6) $$\bar{X}_t = (1 + g - \eta)\bar{X}_{t-1} + \eta X_{t-1} \quad (g = .03).$$

Cagan and Friedman have utilized the continuous analogue of (6). They then made additional assumptions to obtain the estimates from discrete sums. For present purposes the discrete equation is probably a closer approximation to real conditions, in that knowledge of the returns earned by firms only becomes available at the discrete intervals associated with accounting periods.

Equation (6) is a first-order difference equation, the solution to which is

(7) $$\bar{X}_t = (1 + g - \eta)^t \bar{X}_0 + \eta \sum_{i=1}^{t} (1 + g - \eta)^{i-1} X_{t-i}$$

where the appropriate value of the parameter η is determined as that value which maximizes the fit of the model to the data.[8]

An alternative calculation of $\bar{X}_t$ which makes direct use of the expectations model of (6) is also possible. Assume that in an initial year,

---

[6] The properties of equation (5) are examined by J. F. Muth, "Optimal Properties of Exponentially Weighted Forecasts," *Journal of the American Statistical Association*, 1960, pp. 299–306.

[7] Cf. M. Friedman, *A Theory of the Consumption Function*, p. 144.

[8] The degree to which the model "fits" the data is indicated by the coefficient of multiple determination, $\bar{R}^2$. This statistic measures the explanatory power of a regression equation. $\bar{R}^2 = 1 - \sigma_u^2/\sigma_y^2$ [σ_y^2 is the variance of the dependent variable (in our case, investment) and σ_u^2 is the variance of the residuals from the regression equation.] Thus σ_u^2 is the "unexplained" variance in the dependent variable, and $\bar{R}^2$ gives the proportion of total variance explained by the model tested. In making our tests, various values of η are tried. The particular value is selected which maximizes $\bar{R}^2$, i.e., "maximizes the fit,"

$t = 0$, expectations were accurate, such that $\bar{X}_0 = X_0$. The value of $\bar{X}_t$ for succeeding years can then be obtained directly from sequential applications of (6) for specified values of η, the initial year, and the time series X_t. This method was used in estimating $\bar{X}_t$ in the tests reported below.[9]

The time series X_t, the actual dollar return on assets, was taken as the sum of before-tax profits and the interest payments on debt for all corporations. Since nonincorporated businesses have, by definition, no equity securities outstanding in the market, it was necessary to limit the measure of ρ_t to that relevant to corporations only. The implied assumption is that the average measure of ρ_t from corporate data is also relevant to the investment of unincorporated business. The error introduced by this assumption is unknown, but it is probably small in the aggregate measure used.

In order to simplify notation, we will denote the expected yield on assets as $\rho(\eta)_t$, where the argument η is the value of the expectation parameter used in obtaining $\bar{X}_t$ from (6). This parameter η is capable of two interpretations. *First,* as noted, it serves as an index of the extent to which businessmen revise expectations on the basis of present experience. *Second,* by formulating the derivation of profit expectations as in equation (7), it may be seen that η provides us with information on how far backward businessmen look when forming expectations. Following Muth,[10] assume $0 < \eta < 1$ and omit the growth parameter, g. Equation (7) can then be rewritten as[11]

$$(8) \qquad \bar{X}_t = \eta \sum_{i=1}^{t} (1 - \eta)^{i-1} X_{t-i}.$$

Thus, expected profits in period t are simply a weighted average of past profits, since, for large t,

$$(9) \qquad \eta \sum_{i=1}^{t} (1 - \eta)^{i-1} \approx 1.$$

---

[9] In the estimating procedure, 1913 is taken as the base year, in which the expectations are assumed to have been accurately realized. The basis of this selection is partly arbitrary, partly because the time series is relatively constant at this time (so that profit expectations are more likely to have been correct than in years when profits have shown marked variability), and partly because it is felt that the quality of the data becomes more and more questionable prior to this date.

[10] *Op. cit.*

[11] The first term on the right-hand side of equation (7) will vanish as t increases for $g = 0$ and $0 < \eta < 1$.

Utilizing equation (9), define

Median Lag = the number of years elapsing before the accumulated weights are greater than or equal
to .5; and

Total Lag = the number of years elapsing before the accumulated weights are greater than or equal
to .99.

The median and total lags for some representative values of η are
shown in Table 1. To anticipate what follows, when we test various

TABLE 1

η	Median Lag	Total Lag
.05	14	90
.10	7	44
.15	5	29
.18	4	24
.20	4	21
.30	2	13
.50	1	7
.80	1	3

versions of our model, we shall find that the optimal values of η fall
within a range of from .15 to .20. From Table 1, η-values of this magnitude imply that, when forming expectations, (1) businessmen look
back, on the "average," from four to five years, and (2) the experience
of the preceding two and a half decades or so is relevant to them.

A4. r_t: Interest Rates. Interest rates were taken as the average
rate on interest paid on the outstanding bonds of corporations, as compiled by Moody's Investors Service.

A5. K_t: Capital Stock. The problems involved in measuring the
stock of capital have been widely discussed.[12] One obvious conclusion

---

[12] E.g., J. Robinson, "The Production Function and the Theory of Capital,"
Review of Economic Studies, Vol. 21, 1953–54, and the comment by R. M. Solow in
Vol. 23, pp. 101–108. Also, E. F. Denison, "Theoretical Aspects of Quality Change,
Capital Consumption, and Net Capital Formation," pp. 215–261 in *Problems of
Capital Formation*, Vol. 19 of Studies in Income and Wealth, N.B.E.R., 1957.

that can be drawn from this lengthy controversy is that any measure obtained using the crude devices now at our disposal must be regarded as tenuous at best.

Two alternative estimates are employed in this study. The first is that given by Goldsmith and is denoted as K_t^G. This series of estimates is based on straight-line depreciation of each year's investment, assuming an average service life for several different classes of capital goods.

However, an alternative estimate of the capital stock based not on straight-line nominal depreciation but rather upon a distribution of retirements around average service life is suggested and used by the Machinery and Allied Products Institute (MAPI).[13] This method utilizes survival percentages derived from distribution functions which are symmetric around the average service lives of plant and equipment separately. It was applied to the investment data used in this study, and the resulting estimate of the capital stock will be denoted as K_t^M.

A6. Price Deflator. Finally, a price deflator is necessary to put the estimates of I_t, W_t, and K_t in constant dollars.[14] Examination of the available deflators for capital expenditures reveals several deficiencies.[15] In particular, the available indices of equipment costs apparently measure the changing price of a unit of equipment, not the changing price of a unit of productive capacity, in which we are interested. Thus, they do not reflect the change in the productive efficiency of equipment over time.[16] Similarly, construction cost indices measure units of *input* costs and thus make no allowance for either the change in productive ability of new materials or a change in the efficiency of the construction operation itself. The construction cost indices thus include a bias over and above that inherent in the equipment cost indices.

---

[13] *Sixty Years of Capital Formation* (1960), MAPI, Statistical Notes, p. 2. Their analysis is based on the study by R. Winfrey, *Statistical Analysis of Industrial Property Retirements*, Iowa Engineering Experiment Station, Bulletin 125.

[14] Recall that in Chapter 3 the desired stock of capital (equation 47) and, thus, the investment equation (62) are derived in real terms.

[15] E.g., MAPI's Supplement to *Sixty Years of Capital Formation*, Part II, and R. A. Gordon, "Differential Changes in the Prices of Consumers' and Capital Goods," *American Economic Review*, 1961, pp. 937–957 (esp. pp. 941–945).

[16] This bias is thought to be very great by MAPI, which estimates, for example, that the productive capacity of machine tools nearly doubled in the decade and a half after World War II.

Since any attempt to incorporate a correction to eliminate these biases in the present deflators would, at best, be quite crude,[17] an alternative method of deflating, used by MAPI, is employed here. This alternative abandons the attempt to measure changes in the "physical volume" of operations. Instead, estimates are obtained of "changes in *real investment* from year to year, this being defined as investment in dollars of constant purchasing power."[18] The deflated figures thereby reflect changes in real input, not changes in the results of investment. The deflator used herein is, thus, the broadest available measure of changes in the purchasing power of the dollar, the Department of Commerce "implicit" deflator for the privately produced gross national product, with 1954 taken as the base year.

The unit of measurement of investment, wealth, and the capital stock is billions of dollars. Interest rates and the expected yield on assets are measured in percentage terms.

B. Statistical Findings: 1915–1940, 1946–1961

B1. Methodological Problems. Many important methodological problems arise when one attempts to test empirically a hypothesis in the manner employed here. Several are particularly relevant to the tests of the present model. A brief discussion of four of these problems and their effects will help us interpret the results of our tests.

The investment relation given in equation (1) and its variants introduced below are tested in this and the succeeding section by single-equation, least-squares regression techniques. It is assumed that:

(i) the observations on the independent variables in these regression equations are nonstochastic constants; they are thus uncorrelated with each other and are independent of the disturbances u_t;

(ii) the stochastic elements u_t are distributed independently with a finite variance and a zero mean; and

(iii) the functional relationship is linear, as shown in Chapter 3.

---

[17] An attempt to measure the change in the productive efficiency of the aggregate capital stock was made by R. M. Solow, "Technological Change and the Aggregate Production Function," *Review of Economics and Statistics*, 1957, pp. 412–420, and "Comment" by P. Hogan, 1958, pp. 407–413. The admittedly rough nature of the resulting estimates indicates that any such correction would be exceedingly difficult to make.

[18] MAPI supplement, Part II, *op. cit.*

Under these conditions, the parameter estimates given by the regression coefficients are the best linear unbiased estimates obtainable. For the purposes of testing the statistical significance of the estimates obtained, we assume also that the distribution which the disturbances follow is normal.

B1.a. Collinearity. When two of the independent variables in a regression equation are correlated with each other, assumption (i) above is violated. In this case, the theoretically independent effects of these variables cannot be separated because they have moved jointly in the sample over which the test is being made. Although it is possible to estimate the joint effect of the two variables together, it is impossible to identify the effects of one of the variables alone. However, the estimate of the standard error of the total equation, and thus of the index of multiple determination, R^2, is unaffected.[19]

We have found that our measures of capital (K_t) and wealth (W_t) are highly collinear. Thus, the coefficients of these variables must be regarded with caution. Nonetheless, although this collinearity will hamper our efforts at obtaining precise estimates of the investment elasticities of these variables, it will not affect interpretation of the explanatory power of the entire equation. Of course, this latter criterion is one of the more important by which the validity of our model can be judged.

B1.b. Autocorrelated Disturbances. Assumption (ii) above requires that the u_t be distributed independently [i.e., $E(u_t, u_{t+s}) = 0, s \neq 0$]. If the u_t are autocorrelated, three consequences ensue.[20] *First*, although the estimates of the regression coefficients remain unbiased, it is no longer true that the least-squares technique assures a minimum sampling variance attached to these estimates. *Second*, it is likely that the usual formulae will underestimate this sampling variance, thereby exaggerating the statistical significance of the coefficients obtained. *Third*, predictions made from regression equations with autocorrelated disturb-

---

[19] Cf. T. Haavelmo, "Remarks on Frisch's Confluence Analysis and its Use in Econometrics," Chap. 5 in T. J. Koopmans, ed., *Statistical Inference in Dynamic Economic Models*, John Wiley & Sons, Inc., New York, 1950.

[20] Cf., e.g., J. Johnston, *Econometric Methods*, McGraw-Hill, Inc., New York, 1963, Chap. 7.

ances will have sampling variances larger than those which can be obtained if condition (ii) is fulfilled.

These effects do not appear to be overly important in our tests, although positive autocorrelation of the residuals is indicated in tests of the long-run model. To anticipate results given below, virtually all our tests show statistical significance even at an extremely low probability of a Type I error. It is improbable that corrections for autocorrelation would reverse our conclusions at reasonable levels of statistical significance.[21] Also, many of our tests are designed to show the stability of the regression coefficients over time, and the consistency of the coefficients of $\rho(\eta)_t$ and r_t. Since regression coefficients are unbiased, these results will be substantially unaffected. Finally, when short-term considerations are brought into the model, autocorrelation in the disturbance disappears. Since it is this latter model which is used for forecasting purposes in Part D, our predictions can be construed to have been made without loss of statistical efficiency.

Tests for the presence of autocorrelated disturbances in the regression equations below are made with the Durbin-Watson "d" statistic. Let

u_t = the residual from the regression equation for year t

$(t = 1, 2, \ldots, n)$;

$\Delta u_t = u_t - u_{t-1} \ (t = 2, 3, \ldots, n)$.

Then the d statistic is defined as

$$d = \frac{\sum_{t=2}^{n} (\Delta u_t)^2}{\sum_{t=1}^{t} u_t^2}.$$

Exact significance levels are not available, but tables have been prepared giving upper and lower bounds of d for several levels of significance,

---

[21] The basis for this statement is twofold. A rough application of Wold's correction for autocorrelation, as interpreted by M. Ezekiel and K. A. Fox, *Methods of Correlation and Regression Analysis*, 3rd. ed., John Wiley & Sons, Inc., New York, 1959, p. 335, indicates that the degree of autocorrelation found in our tests is not important enough to jeopardize our conclusions. This finding was supported by a statistical analyst concerned with this problem at the National Bureau of Economic Research (private conversation).

given the number of observations and the number of independent variables.[22]

B1.c. Errors of Measurement. When the observations of the variables in a regression equation contain errors of measurement, assumption (i) is again violated, and the estimate of both the regression coefficient and the partial correlation coefficient for that variable will contain a downward bias. Thus, these coefficients will appear, aside from sampling fluctuations, smaller than the true value.[23]

Though virtually all economic statistics undoubtedly contain some errors of measurement, the variables in our equation that are most subject to these errors are K_t, $\rho(\eta)_t$, and r_t. Difficulty in interpreting the coefficient of K_t was already discussed above because of the multi-collinearity problem.

Our limited ability to measure expectations is widely known, and it would be redundant to further discuss these limitations in the present context. That our measure of $\rho(\eta)_t$ contains errors of measurement is certain; we can only argue that the procedure we have used to measure this variable has been successful in other applications, and that it appears plausible that the expectations model we have employed does represent at least part of the basic process by which expectations are formed. To the extent that errors are introduced by the measurement process used, the estimate of the regression coefficient will be biased downward.

---

[22] J. Durbin and G. S. Watson, "Testing for Serial Correlation in Least-Squares Regression," *Biometrika*, 1950 (Part I) and 1951 (Part II).

Given the upper (d_U) and the lower (d_L) bounds of d, the decision as to the presence of autocorrelation in the disturbances is made as follows:

| | Autocorrelation: | |
	Positive	Negative
Significant:	$d < d_L$	$4 - d < d_L$
Nonsignificant:	$d > d_U$	$4 - d > d_U$
Inconclusive:	$d_L < d < d_U$	$d_L < 4 - d < d_U$

If there is no autocorrelation in the residuals, $d = 2$. If there is perfect *positive* autocorrelation, $d = 0$. If there is perfect negative autocorrelation, $d = 4$.

[23] Cf. two articles with the same title, "The Fitting of Straight Lines If Both Variables Are Subject To Error"; M. S. Bartlett, *Biometrics*, 1949, pp. 207–242; A. Madansky, *Journal of the American Statistical Association*, 1959, pp. 173–205. Also, A. Hald, *Statistical Theory with Engineering Applications*, John Wiley & Sons, Inc., New York, 1952, pp. 615–616, and J. Johnston, *Econometric Methods*, McGraw-Hill, Inc., New York, 1963, chap. 6.

Our measure of r_t undoubtedly also contains such errors. As mentioned in Chapter 2, the measure we are using does not incorporate the elements of capital cost inherent in some of the practices of lending institutions. For example, the requirement of compensating balances increases the true, although unreported, cost of borrowing a given amount of funds, and this effect is not included in the present measure. To the extent that these errors of measurement are independent of true interest costs, both the estimate of the regression coefficient and its statistical significance will be downward biased.

B1.d. Retesting. As mentioned in the previous section, our estimate of the parameter η in the variable $\rho(\eta)_t$ will be selected as that value which maximizes the fit of the model to the data. We use as our criterion for this purpose the value of R^2, which measures the proportion of the variance in the dependent variable which is explained by the regression plane. Thus, the regression equations presented below are the result of many retests on a particular form of the equation, a separate test having been run on approximately twenty-five values of η.

Any test is bound to show statistical significance if redone enough times. In fact, by the definition of the Type I error (α), a test may be expected *a priori* to show significant deviations from the null hypothesis $100\ \alpha$ per cent of the time even if the null hypothesis is true. We must ask, then, if our results are truly significant or if the indicated significance is merely the result of many retests.

If, in the extreme case, each retest was made independently, then the probability of correctly rejecting the null hypothesis would be $1 - \alpha$ for each individual test run, and the joint probability of a correct decision for the n tests together would be $(1 - \alpha)^n$. The probability of erroneously rejecting the null hypothesis after n trials, α_n, would be

$$\alpha_n = 1 - (1 - \alpha)^n.$$

Thus, if $n = 25$ and $\alpha = .05$, then the true chance of erroneously accepting the alternative hypothesis, α_n, would be approximately .72. The value of alpha on each individual test which would be needed to lower α_n to .05 would be .002.

Of course, to the extent that each retest is dependent on a previous test, α_n (the probability of rejecting the null hypothesis erroneously) would be reduced drastically. In our case, this is most certainly true. The underlying data are exactly the same from test to test and we are merely searching the two-dimensional space defined by $(\eta,\ \bar{R}^2)$ for that point with the maximum ordinate. The other conditions of the test remain the same.[24]

If our $\bar{R}^2$ is statistically significant at $\alpha = .002$, we are assured that we have completely corrected for any bias which might have been introduced inadvertently by the procedure for obtaining $\rho(\eta)$. It is perhaps worth mentioning here that the values of $\bar{R}^2$ which we find, do indeed indicate statistical significance at and beyond even this ultraconservative level of α. Thus, the results obtained are not invalidated by the use of numerical methods.

B2. The Basic Model. The least-squares regression estimate of equation (1) using the two alternative measures of the capital stock gives the following results:

(10) $I_t = -6.629 + .0486W_t + 1.096[\rho(.205) - r]_t + .0380K_t^G,$

"t" values   (5.78)   (13.23)   (3.55)

$$\bar{R}^2 = .947, \qquad d = 1.02;$$

(11) $I_t = -6.659 + .0547W_t + 1.183[\rho(.180) - r]_t + .0224K_t^M,$

"t" values   (6.23)   (11.39)   (2.42)

$$\bar{R}^2 = .944, \qquad d = 1.01.$$

The values of Student's "t" statistic (the absolute value of the ratio of the coefficient to its standard error) are included in parentheses directly below the regression coefficients.

Several points deserve comment. *First*, the fit of the model to the data, as indicated by $\bar{R}^2$ (corrected for degrees of freedom) is quite good. This is definite evidence in support of the theoretical considerations advanced in the preceding chapter, and indicates that further study of the properties of the model is indeed a worthwhile undertaking.

In this case, a significant value of $\bar{R}^2$ cannot be taken as final evidence of the explanatory properties of the model. The mutual growth in the dependent and independent variables can be construed as the result of movements in another variable which is exogenous to the equation being tested. Hence, it is important to examine the alternative hypothesis that the variance in the investment series can be explained by trend alone.

---

[24] Investigation indicated both that the relationship between $\bar{R}^2$ and η was essentially unimodal and that the function was relatively flat in the area of the maximum. Cf. footnote 33.

A regression of investment on time yields:[25]

(12) $I_t = -6.112 + .588(t - 1900),$

"t" value   (11.84)

$$\bar{r}^2 = .772, \qquad d = 0.29.$$

Approximately 77 per cent of the variance in investment can be explained by trend. Our model, however, explained approximately 95 per cent. Thus, the partial correlation of our model, given the prior effect of trend,[26] is 0.88. This is significant at extremely small levels of significance,[27] and is again a quite satisfactory measure.

Second, while the coefficients of wealth, yield, and—by implication[28]—interest rates are as expected, the sign of the coefficient of the capital stock is contrary to the specification of the model. As previously noted by both Klein and Grunfeld, economically this may simply indicate that in the partial relationship between gross investment and the capital stock, the (positive) "replacement effect" outweighs the (negative) "net investment" effect.[29]

However, this result may be explained on statistical grounds alone without invoking any economic considerations. In the first place, the presence of serial correlation in the residuals is indicated by the value

---

[25] The time span is identical to that used in the other tests of this and the next section (i.e., 1915–1940, 1946–1961).

[26] Partial correlation is defined as the square root of the proportion of residual variance explained, or, in this case,

$$\sqrt{\frac{.95 - .77}{1. - .77}} = .88.$$

Cf. R. A. Fisher, *Statistical Methods for Research Workers*, 13th ed., Hafner Publishing Co., Inc., New York, 1958, Chap. 6.

[27] The statistic for testing the significance of a correlation coefficient is normally distributed with zero mean and unit variance and is defined as

$$u = \frac{1}{2}\left(\ln \frac{1 + r}{1 - r}\right)\sqrt{f},$$

where $f = n' - 3$. For a total correlation coefficient, $n' = n$, the number of observations. For a partial correlation coefficient, $n' = n - e$, where e is the number of variables eliminated. The value of u for $r = .88$ is $1.375\sqrt{38} = 8.47$, which is significant beyond $\alpha = 10^{-6}$.

[28] An explicit test of the sign of the coefficient of the interest rate variable is conducted in section B4, below.

[29] Cf. Chapter 3, section B.2.

of d,[30] indicating that the estimated standard errors of the regression coefficients may be slightly underestimated. Thus, the coefficients of the capital stock may not be statistically significant. Of more importance, however, is the fact that there is definite indication of the presence of multicollinearity between K_t and W_t.[31] Although in principle these variables are different, over the period examined their movements are sufficiently correlated so that our separate estimates of the coefficients of these two variables are statistically unreliable.

For all these reasons, plus the fact mentioned earlier that very little confidence can be put in the obtainable measures of the capital stock, some additional assumptions are introduced. These permit an alternative of the model which avoids some of these difficulties.

B3. The Basic Model Eliminating the Capital Stock. Assume that K_t is a linear function of W_t,

$$(13) \qquad\qquad K_t = a + bW_t.$$

Then, by substitution of (13) into (1) we obtain

$$(14) \qquad I_t = \alpha_0' + \alpha_1' W_t + \alpha_2 [\rho(\eta) - r]_t + u_t,$$

where

$$\alpha_0' = \alpha_0 + \alpha_3 a,$$

$$\alpha_1' = \alpha_1 + \alpha_3 b.$$

and the coefficient of $[\rho(\eta) - r]_t$ should remain unchanged.

Excluding the capital stock variable in this manner from equations (6) and (7), the regression obtained is

$$(15) \qquad I_t = -5.921 + .0736W_t + 1.605[\rho(.155) - r]_t,$$

"t" values $\qquad\qquad\qquad\quad (18.54) \qquad\ (21.59)$

$$\bar{R}^2 = .947, \qquad d = 1.03.$$

---

[30] The critical lower bound for d for 42 observations and 3 independent variables at a level of significance of .05 using a one-tailed test is approximately 1.35. A test value of d below this may be taken as evidence of the presence of positive serial correlation.

[31] The simple correlation coefficients between W_t and K_t^G, between W_t and K_t^M, are .72 and .67 respectively. Both of these values are significant beyond the .0001 level, using Fisher's test.

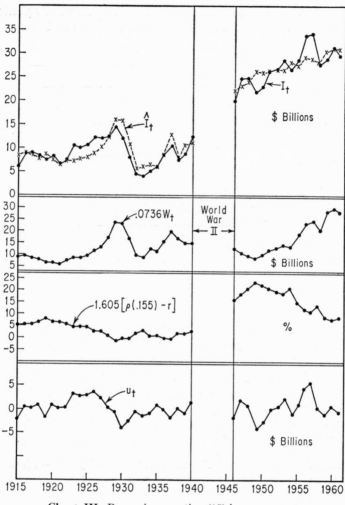

Chart III. Regression equation (15) by component

The explanation of the investment series provided by equation (15) is shown graphically by component in Chart III. A comparison of equation (15) with (11) and (12) reveals that there is no loss in explanatory power caused by excluding the capital stock.[32] In addition, the validity

---

[32] The insignificant increase in $\bar{R}^2$ in (15) relative to (11) can be explained in terms of the change in the correction of degrees of freedom caused by the elimination of an independent variable.

of assumptions (13) and (14) can be demonstrated. Regressions of K_t^G and K_t^M on W_t give the following estimates for a and b:

	a	b
K^M	127.818	.745
K^G	78.091	.588

Employing the estimates of α_0, α_1, and α_3 from (10) and (11) along with these estimates of a and b according to the definitions in (14) we obtain the following estimates of α_0' and α_1':

	Eq. (10)	Eq. (11)	actual [Eq. (15)]
α_0'	−3.662	−3.796	−5.921
α_1'	.0809	.0714	.0736

Thus, the estimates of the constant term (α_0') are of the correct magnitude and the deviations from (α_1') can be explained in terms of sampling variation. We conclude that the changes in these two coefficients are consistent with our procedure.

The change in the coefficient of $[\rho(\eta) - r]_t$ resulting from the exclusion of the capital stock involves a more complicated explanation. An examination of sequential runs of the regression equation reveals that there is a substantial negative relationship between the value of the expectations parameter η and the regression coefficient of $\rho(\eta)_t$. In terms of the fit of the model to the data, there is apparently a substitution between this coefficient and η, since the change in $\bar{R}^2$ for a rather wide relative range of values of is quite small.[33] Thus, the change

---

[33] E.g., the changes in both $\bar{R}^2$ and the coefficient of $[\rho(\eta) - r]_t$ for various values of η, other things remaining the same, are as follows:

η	$\bar{R}^2$	Coefficient of $[\rho(\eta) - r]_t$
.125	.9443	1.882
.135	.9461	1.741
.145	.9471	1.669
.150	.9473	1.636
.155	.9475*	1.605
.160	.9474	1.576
.170	.9471	1.524
.185	.9462	1.455

*optimum: equation (15)

Thus, for changes in η of ±20 per cent from $\eta^* = .155$, the change in $\bar{R}^2$ is trivial.

in the coefficient of $[\rho(\eta) - r]_t$ when the capital stock is excluded may be viewed as caused by two effects: (a) a change in the values of $\rho(\eta)_t$ resulting from the change in the value of η (the "parameter effect"), and (b) a change in the partial relationship between investment and $[\rho(\eta) - r]_t$ caused by the exclusion of capital (the "exclusion effect"). By hypothesis [i.e., equations (13) and (14)], this exclusion effect should not exist.

Identification of the strengths of these two effects can be made by examining the change in the coefficients of $[\rho(\eta) - r]_t$ from (10) and (11) to (15) while keeping η constant. The resulting change may then be viewed as the exclusion effect while the remaining change is the parameter effect.

When fixing η at .155 [the optimum value in (15)], the value of the coefficient of $[\rho(\eta) - r]_t$ is 1.461, using K_t^G ($\bar{R}^2 = .943$) and 1.466, using K_t^M ($\bar{R}^2 = .941$). Thus, the "exclusion effect" accounts for only one-third of the total change. This amount is well within the range of sampling variation, as given by the standard error of the coefficient. Thus, there is no significant change in α_2 introduced by elimination of the capital stock.

It appears, then, that the primary effect of eliminating the capital stock from the statistical estimates of the relationships between the variables of the model is to alter the parameter estimate of the wealth coefficient. Since we are unable to put confidence in our measures of K_t, because of the presence of multicollinearity, and because the other conclusions we draw from further tests of the model will not be basically affected by its exclusion, we will continue to eliminate the capital stock in the remainder of the tests of this chapter.

B4. Yields and Interest Rates. In the course of deriving the investment equation implied by the theoretical model of the firm in the preceding chapter, one of the properties of this investment relation was found to be that the coefficients of the yield variable $\rho(\eta)_t$ should have the same order of magnitude as, but a sign opposite to that of, the coefficient of interest costs, r_t. Thus, a further test of the model is provided by seeing whether this property holds.

When the variables $\rho(\eta)_t$ and r_t are entered separately into the regression equation, the results are

(16) $I_t = -7.347 + .0747 W_t + 1.644\rho(.155)_t - 1.432r_t,$

"t" values   (16.47)   (16.25)   (4.57)

$$\bar{R}^2 = .946, \qquad d = 1.03.$$

Thus, the results again support the model. *First*, the coefficients of $\rho(\eta)_t$ and r_t differ only by a margin which is totally explainable in terms of sampling variation.[34] *Second*, the η which yields the highest $\bar{R}^2$ is unchanged from that of equation (15), where the effects of $\rho(\eta)_t$ and r_t were combined into a single variable. *Third*, there is no difference in the fit of the model from equation (15) to (16), indicating that the effects of the two variables did enter separately into the results of equation (15).[35] *Fourth*, there is no statistically significant change in the marginal propensity to invest with respect to wealth. Thus, the data provide strong support for this implication of the hypothesis.

Note that interest rates enter negatively and significantly into the investment equation. Previous models (e.g., Tinbergen, Klein, Modigliani and Kisselgoff, Meyer and Kuh) have failed to show the significant role of interest rates. Their failure to do so has been widely interpreted as suggesting that investment expenditures have no significant interest elasticity and, thus, that monetary policy is rendered impotent in its attempt to affect the level of investment in fixed capital.

We take the failure of earlier models to show significant interest rate effects as resulting from two primary factors. *First*, previous models have improperly specified the constraint with respect to which the firm's investment decisions are made. As we have seen, this role is given to the wealth constraint in the present model. *Second*, the profits variable should not enter the equation in *absolute* magnitudes, but should, instead, enter as a yield.[36] This conclusion originates in the theoretical development of Chapter 3 and is supported by statistical investigation. Thus, the statistical evidence gathered by econometricians, which indicates the ineffectiveness of interest rates on investment decisions, re-

---

[34] The value of the t-statistic used to test the difference between two coefficients is

$$t = \frac{\hat{b}_1 = \hat{b}_2}{(\text{Var } (\hat{b}_1) + \text{Var } (\hat{b}_2) - 2 \text{ Cor } (\hat{b}_1, \hat{b}_2))^{1/2}} = .83$$

which, of course, is nonsignificant.

[35] The value of the $F(38, 39)$ statistic is $s^2(16)/s^2(15) = 1.01$, which indicates no statistical difference in the fit of equation (16) from equation (15).

[36] It is interesting that while the theoretical considerations underlying the Klein-Goldberger model favor the measurement of profits as a yield (following the approach used in the present model), profits were entered as an absolute amount solely because of the desire to maintain linearity in the relations tested, a requirement of the statistical technique used to estimate the coefficients of a large, simultaneous multi-equation model. Thus, the Klein-Goldberger formulation of the profits variable may be taken as a result of our limited knowledge of statistical, not economic theory. A more detailed investigation of their model will be included in Part D below.

sults from an improper formulation of the investment function and can be seriously called into question.

Of course, while our theoretical development indicates that wealth and interest rates play critical roles in the investment process, the variable on which the asset-allocating mechanism fundamentally depends is expected yield. We can examine the extent to which mis-specification of the constraint (or other variables) in previous studies of the investment function has led to errors in interpreting the effect of interest rates on investment. In equations (17) and (18) the model is intentionally mis-specified. Both $\rho(\eta)_t$ and r_t are eliminated separately from the equation to test the relevance of wealth and yields for an understanding of the determinants of investment:

Exclude r_t:

(17) $\qquad I_t = -15.644 + .0816W_t + 1.639\rho(.190)_t,$

"*t*" values $\qquad\qquad\qquad$ (16.58) $\qquad$ (17.27)

$$\bar{R}^2 = .920, \qquad d = 0.71;$$

Exclude $\rho(\eta)_t$:

(18) $\qquad I_t = 25.130 + .0469W_t - 3.842r_t,$

"*t*" values $\qquad\qquad\qquad$ (4.01) $\qquad$ (5.01)

$$\bar{R}^2 = .586, \qquad d = 0.22.$$

Thus, while the model still performs respectably when interest rates are excluded, it performs poorly when $\rho(\eta)_t$ is eliminated. Note that in equation (18) interest rates still enter the equation negatively and significantly, indicating that when the budget constraint is properly specified, the negative effect of interest rates on investment remains critical even when expected yields are omitted from consideration. Note further that the constant term in (18) becomes positive, reflecting the positive effect of the omitted variable, while the constant term becomes much more negative in (17), reflecting the omission of r_t.

Also, from equations (17) and (15), the partial correlation of interest rates and investment, given the prior effects of wealth and yield, can be calculated. This partial correlation is found to be .61, and is significant beyond the .001 level.[37] Thus, interest rates must be considered

---

[37] The partial correlation coefficient is $\sqrt{\dfrac{.95 - .92}{1.00 - .92}} = .61.$

an important determinant of the level of investment. Further discussion of interest rates and their role in economic activity is included in Chapter 5.

B5. Structural Stability. Another test of the long-term applicability of the model is provided by asking whether the equation has been reasonably stable over time. Indeed, in Chapter 2 it was argued that if the rationality hypothesis is correct and the model of the decision situation is correctly conceived, then although the detailed procedures by which decisions are made may change as new techniques become available and in vogue, the results of these decisions, as captured by the regression estimates of the parameters in the equation, should provide relatively stable relationships between the causal variables and investment expenditures.

A test of this stability has been made by dividing the period for which data had been obtained into two subperiods, prewar (1915–1940) and postwar (1946–1961). Of course, because of the great loss in degrees of freedom resulting from this split of the original data into subperiods, we should not place too much confidence in the standard errors of the coefficients (which are really estimates strictly valid only for large samples). Also, the influence of short-term effects will be of greater relative importance in these shorter subperiods than in the period as a whole. Therefore, we would not expect that the fit of the model, which is oriented toward long-term considerations, will be as close to the data in the subperiods. What we are primarily interested in when we use this test is the stability of the relationships between the variables, i.e., the stability of the estimates of the coefficients themselves.

Using that value of η which again maximizes the fit of the equation to the data, we obtain the following results:

Prewar: 1915–1940 (optimum η)

(19) $\qquad I_t = -0.821 + .0493W_t + 1.066[\rho(.200) - r]_t,$

"t" values $\qquad\qquad\qquad$ (6.03) $\qquad\quad$ (4.08)

$$\bar{R}^2 = .584, \qquad d = 0.60;$$

Postwar: 1946–1961 (optimum η)

(20) $\qquad I_t = -1.119 + .0694W_t + 1.202[\rho(.160) - r]_t,$

"t" values $\qquad\qquad\qquad$ (2.70) $\qquad\quad$ (1.57)

$$\bar{R}^2 = .592, \qquad d = 1.23.$$

While well over half the variance in the investment series is still explained by the model in these subperiods, the coefficient of multiple determination is, as expected, decreased. This reduction in explanatory power of the model is most likely due to the effects of short-term variations, which will have more importance as the length of the period examined is shortened.

We note also that the primary change between (19), (20), and (15) is that the coefficient of $[\rho(\eta) - r]_t$ is lower in the subperiods, particularly for the prewar, than in the period as a whole. This change can again be separated into two effects, one resulting from a change in the parameter η and the other from a change in the relationship itself. From equation (5), the parameter η is a "coefficient of expectations" which measures the degree to which long-run expectations are revised due to short-term changes. Since it is evident that η is slightly larger in both of the subperiods than in the complete period, this evidence suggests that economic expectations are based on the more recent past and that they are more volatile in the short run than over longer periods.

To examine the extent to which the regression coefficient of $[\rho(\eta) - r]_t$ has changed due to the change in η, we constrain η to its optimum value in (15), which was .155. The results of the subperiod analysis in this case are:

Prewar: 1915–1940 ($\eta = .155$)

$$(21) \qquad I_t = -3.549 + .0592W_t + 1.549[\rho(.155) - r]_t,$$

"t" values   (5.51)   (3.82)

$$\bar{R}^2 = .562, \qquad d = 0.65;$$

Postwar: 1946–1961 ($\eta = .155$)

$$(22) \qquad I_t = -.899 + .0694W_t + 1.206[\rho(.155) - r]_t,$$

"t" values   (2.71)   (1.57)

$$\bar{R}^2 = .592, \qquad d = 1.23.$$

Thus, the equations are seen to exhibit remarkable stability between the two subperiods examined when the expectations parameter remains constant, and this in spite of the great social, political, and economic changes that occurred during these years.[38] We take this as further evidence that our model provides us with a proper first approximation within which to view the investment decision, at least at aggregative levels.

The structural stability found in our model has relevance to a point frequently raised by economists when discussing the conditions that prevailed during the 1930's. During the Depression, it has been argued that the system collapsed, and the relationships which existed in more normal years broke down during this period. Of course, we are only concerned with one equation of the total economic system, and, thus, any conclusions which we might be able to reach about this investment relation

---

[38] A statistical comparison of equations (21) and (22) reveals that no statistically significant difference exists between them. The test of equality between the sets of coefficients in the two equations is that given by J. Johnston, *Econometric Methods*, McGraw-Hill, Inc., New York, 1963, pp. 136–138. Let β_i be the estimated set of regression coefficients for the ith equation ($i = 1, 2$), corresponding to our equations (21) and (22). We test the hypothesis that $\beta_1 = \beta_2 = \beta_3$, where β_3 is the joint estimate of the regression coefficients obtained by pooling all the data [i.e., the coefficients of equation (15)]. Then, if the disturbances in equations (21) and (22) have the same variance of extimate s_i^2 the hypothesis may be tested by computing the F ratio,

$$F = \frac{(Q_1 - Q_2)/k}{Q_2/(m + n - 2k)},$$

where

n = number of observations in the first equation (or 26);

m = number of observations in the second equation (or 16);

k = number of coefficients (or 3);

Q_1 = sum of squared residuals obtained by pooling all the data [i.e., from equation (15)] (or 188.8);

Q_2 = the sum of squared residuals for the first equation plus the sum of squared residuals for the second equation (or 157.1).

The hypothesis is rejected if this F-statistic, which has k and $m + n - 2k$ degrees of freedom, is significant.

Thus, we first test if both relations have the same variance of estimate. If the lines are identical, the s_i^2 will be estimates of a common σ^2 and their ratio will be distributed as F. The value of this statistic is 2.12, which, with 13 and 23 degrees of freedom, indicates no significant difference at the .05 level.

We then find that the value of the F-statistic defined above is 2.43. With 3 and 36 degrees of freedom, this value again is not statistically significant. (The critical value of F at the .05 level is 2.86.) Thus, we accept the hypothesis that the sets of regression coefficients in equations (15), (21), and (22) are drawn from the same populations.

should not be taken to necessarily apply to the system as a whole. Nevertheless, the investment equation is an important determinant of the level of income in most models of the economic system. In addition, it is the investment equation which is most often said to be unstable.[39] Hence, evidence of stability of the investment function is of some consequence.

It is interesting to note that during the 1930's the model does not disintegrate but, indeed, does again indicate essentially constant structure:

1930–1939 (optimum η)

(23) $\qquad I_t = -1.248 + .0450W_t + .481[\rho(.175) - r]_t,$

"t" values $\qquad\qquad\qquad$ (7.30) $\qquad$ (1.00)

$$\bar{R}^2 = .887, \qquad d = 0.73;$$

1930–1939 ($\eta = .155$)

(24) $\qquad I_t = -1.759 + .0468W_t + .524[\rho(.155) - r]_t,$

"t" values $\qquad\qquad\qquad$ (6.01) $\qquad$ (.93)

$$\bar{R}^2 = .885, \qquad d = 0.76.$$

Again we find that the optimal $\eta (= .175)$ is higher in this shorter period than in the period as a whole. Also, despite the fact that the short period tested encompasses only a decade, so that short-term fluctuations have a large relative importance, our model explains almost 90 per cent of the variance in investment during the 1930's. Most of this explanation comes from the wealth variable.[40]

Hence, the fact that investment was low during this period may be explained in terms of the model. Wealth fell during the early 30's, interest rates were relatively high (again, especially in the early 30's), and yields were relatively low.[41] The reasons for these phenomena might have to be obtained from a study of the economic system in its entirety.

---

[39] E.g., J. M. Keynes, *The General Theory of Employment, Interest and Money*, p. 315.

[40] The partial correlation of $[\rho(\eta) - r]_t$ with respect to I_t, given the prior effect of W_t, is .3, which has only a 60–40 chance of being significant.

[41] For example, the average of $\rho(.155)$ during the entire sample period was 9.60 per cent; during the 1930's it was 5.11 per cent.

However, an explanation of the level of business investment expenditures which occurred during this period seems to be within the scope of our model.

C. Short-term Considerations

C1. The Effect of Partially Completed Plans.
It was noted in Chapter 3 that on the average we would expect only a fraction γ $(0 < \gamma < 1)$ of the investment desired in a given year actually to be completed [i.e., $I_t = \gamma I_t^D$, equation (53) of Chapter 3]. This is caused by occasional bottlenecks in supply, by planning, engineering, and construction lags, etc. Following Koyck,[42] let us assume that the effect of past uncompleted plans on investment expenditures in year t decreases regularly in geometric proportion, where the factor of proportionality is $1 - \gamma$, so that the accumulated weights sum to unity. Then

$$(25) \qquad I_t = \gamma \sum_{i=0}^{\infty} (1 - \gamma)^i I_{t-i}^D \quad (0 < \gamma < 1).$$

By shifting the equation one period backward, multiplying by $1 - \gamma$, and subtracting from (21), we obtain

$$I_t = \gamma I_t^D + \gamma(1 - \gamma)I_{t-1}^D + \gamma(1 - \gamma)^2 I_{t-2}^D$$
$$+ \gamma(1 - \gamma)^3 I_{t-3}^D \cdots$$

$$(1 - \gamma)I_{t-1} = \gamma(1 - \gamma)I_{t-1}^D + \gamma(1 - \gamma)^2 I_{t-2}^D$$
$$+ \gamma(1 - \gamma)^3 I_{t-3}^D \cdots$$

$$\overline{I_t - (1 - \gamma)I_{t-1} = \gamma I_t^D}$$

or

$$(26) \qquad I_t = \gamma I_t^D + (1 - \gamma)I_{t-1},$$

which is the equation to be tested. The variable I_t^D is, of course, given by equation (52) of Chapter 3.

---

[42] L. M. Koyck, *Distributed Lags and Investment Analysis*, North-Holland Publishing Company, Amsterdam, 1954.

The estimates of equation (26) for 1915–1940, 1946–1961 are shown by (27) and (28). For purposes of comparison, the alternative estimates of the capital stock are added.

(27) $I_t = -3.633 + .0462W_t + .988[\rho(.160) - r]_t,$

"t" values   (4.75)   (5.24)

$$- .0006K_t^G + .393I_{t-1}$$
$$(0.42) \qquad (2.75)$$

$$\bar{R}^2 + .953, \qquad d = 1.21;$$

(28) $I_t = -3.543 + .0482W_t + 1.053[\rho(.145) - r]_t,$

"t" values   (4.69)   (5.33)

$$-.0042K_t^M + .415I_{t-1},$$
$$(.40) \qquad (3.21)$$

$$\bar{R}^2 = .953, \qquad d = 1.22.$$

Thus, although the signs of the estimates of the coefficients of the capital stock are now in the hypothesized direction, these estimates are definitely nonsignificant statistically. For the reasons advanced above, it was decided to eliminate this variable from further tests. Excluding the capital stock from equations (27) and (28), the results are

(29) $I_t = 3.532 + .0459W_t + .985[\rho(.165) - r]_t + .380I_{t-1},$

"t" values   (5.30)   (5.60)   (3.44)

$$\bar{R}^2 = .959, \qquad d = 1.24.$$

This equation is graphed by component in Chart IV.

The coefficient of lagged investment is statistically significant[43] and implies an estimate of γ of .62. While the renewed presence of multicollinearity due to the introduction of lagged investment gives us reason to be properly cautious in our interpretation of this parameter,[44] the

---

[43] The critical lower bound of the d statistic at the 5 per cent level is 1.35. Thus, though there is evidence of a small amount of positive serial correlation, the correction of the standard errors of the coefficients would not be enough to change the conclusions concerning the statistical significance of the estimates.

[44] The simple correlation between lagged investment and wealth is .59; $r_{I_{t-1}}$, $[\rho(.165) - r]_t = .70$.

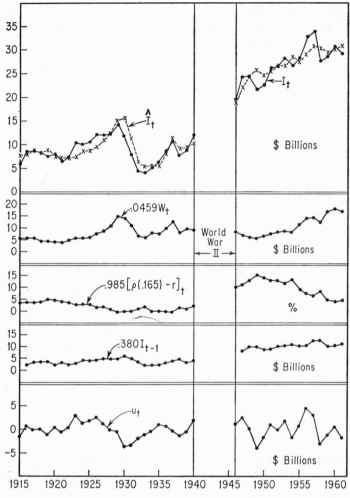

Chart IV. Regression equation (29) by component

evidence supplied by equation (29) does indicate that, on average, better than half of the desired expenditures are completed each year.

The rise in $\bar{R}^2$ in equation (29) from equation (15) implies a partial correlation coefficient for lagged investment, given the prior effects of W_t and $[\rho(\eta) - r]_t$, of .47. This value is significant beyond the .01 level.

It is also interesting that when $\rho(\eta)_t$ and r_t are separated using the model of (26), the conclusions of section B4 remain unchanged. The coefficients of these two variables, within the range of statistical determination,[45] are the same, and the fit of the model to the data is unchanged:

$$(30) \quad I_t = -1.428 + .0417W_t + .881\rho(.165)_t - 1.165r_t + .417I_{t-1},$$

"t" values $\quad\quad\quad$ (4.17) $\quad\quad$ (4.02) $\quad\quad\quad$ (4.09) $\quad\quad$ (3.48)

$$\bar{R}^2 = .958, \quad\quad d = 1.29.$$

The implication of the model, that interest rates and the marginal efficiency of capital are of equal importance, is again strongly supported by these results.

C2. The Effect of Transitory Changes

C2a. Price Changes. The effect of short-term variations in the price of capital (plant and equipment), P_t^K, relative to the price of labor (i.e., the wage rate), P_t^L, was explored.[46] While price changes theoretically should be reflected in expectations [and, thus, in our variable $\rho(\eta)_t$], the *timing* of investment expenditures can still be determined by these short-term factors. In addition, it is entirely possible that the procedure we employed to measure expectations does not adequately incorporate the effects of price changes.

If P_t^K becomes high relative to P_t^L, *ceteris paribus*, labor will be substituted for capital in the production process, and investment expenditures will be either postponed or curtailed. Thus, the observation on the investment series will be low relative to the long-term average given by the line of regression, and the residual (i.e., actual less calculated investment) for that period should be negative.

The residuals of equations (15) and (29) were regressed on the ratio P_t^K/P_t^L. The results showed no significant indication that short-term price changes did affect investment over the period examined. While the signs of the coefficients were in the expected direction, the results were totally nonsignificant, and no firm inferences can be drawn.

---

[45] The t-statistic is 1.41, which indicates no significant difference.

[46] The series on P_t^K was compiled as a weighted average of the separate series on the costs of plant and capital equipment, where the weights are the proportion of total investment undertaken in construction and equipment, respectively. The series on P_t^L is from the series on hourly earnings in manufacturing industries. Both series were converted to indices with 1954 = 100, and are presented in the Appendix.

There are several possible explanations for this null result. *First,* it is possible that the magnitude of the price changes was so small relative to the price of, and the interest payments on capital that their effects were too small to be detected by a broad, aggregative test such as we have made.

Second, while the effect expected in fact may have been operating, a counter force is being applied in the form of higher investment demand, forcing up P_t^K to begin with. Capital prices are not determined independent of the demand for capital. Years in which investment is high, relative to the long-term average "predicted" by the regression equation, and in which the residuals are positive would be exactly those years in which P_t^K would rise. Indeed, we expect that both of these forces are operating simultaneously, and the results might be taken as weak evidence of this fact.

Finally, it is possible that our measure of $\rho(\eta)_t$ does capture much of the short-term price effects which we seek. If so, these effects have already been incorporated in earlier tests. This conclusion would tend to buttress our confidence in the measurement methods employed.

C2.b. Transitory Yield. Another short-run effect which might affect the volume of investment expenditures is represented by transitory profits earned by the firm [i.e., $\bar{X}^T$ in equation (3)]. When actual profits are higher than expected, actual yields will rise above expected yields. This may raise investment. However, it takes time for desired investment plans to be completed. The added incentive to invest may not become evident in the investment statistics of the year in which these transitory profits are experienced. In this case, our model of Chapter 3 need not be considered incomplete in this respect. In addition, transitory profits may be reflected in the investment expenditures of the succeeding year because of planning and construction lags. To the extent that this is so, our measurement of expected yield, which relies on the transitory profits of the preceding year (cf. section A3), already incorporates these effects.

Regressions of the residuals of both equations (15) and (29) show no significant partial correlation between investment and transitory yield.[47] Thus, both our model and the procedures we have followed are justified by this additional test.

---

[47] The partial correlations are .00 and .23 with respect to the residuals of equations (15) and (29) respectively.

C2.c. The Level of General Economic Activity. In Part D of this chapter, the forecasting abilities of several alternative models used to explain investment expenditures are compared. Because the results of forecasts of this type are very dependent on the effects of short-term factors, an attempt is made to find a method by which these forces can be incorporated within the present long-term model and, thus, further reduce the residual variance in the investment series from that left by equation (29).

In particular, an examination of the residuals of (29) reveals the possibility that they are correlated with changes in the general level of economic activity (cf. Chart V). If this is so, then, by adjusting the forecast of the model by some external, known factor which purports to measure and precede changes in general activity, we should be able to increase the forecasting efficiency of the model.

Two tests were made in an effort to ascertain whether these residuals are in fact correlated with "cyclical" movements. *First*, a regression of the residuals of equation (25), u_t^{29}, was run on an index of transitory aggregate income, as defined by Friedman,[48] Y_t^T. The results of the test are as follows:

(31) $$u_t^{29} = -8.914 + 8.194 Y_t^T,$$

"t" value $\qquad\qquad\qquad (2.51)$

$$\bar{r}^2 = .122, \qquad d = 1.28.$$

Thus, this test indicates that transitory aggregate income does exert a significant impact on the volume of invest expenditures.[49]

A *second* measure of movements in aggregate economic activity is provided by the unemployment rate, N_t^u. This measure was used as the independent variable in a regression using u_t^{29} as the dependent variable.

---

[48] Friedman, in *A Theory of the Consumption Function, op. cit.*, defines income, Z, as composed of "permanent," Z^p, and transitory, Z^t, components, similar to our equation (3). Our index of transitory income Y^T is defined as

$$Y^T = \frac{Z}{Z^p} = \frac{Z^p + Z^T}{Z^p} = 1 + \frac{Z^T}{Z^p}.$$

Thus, this index will move above and below unity as transitory income is positive or negative.

[49] Fisher's u-statistic for the correlation coefficient is 2.19 as against a critical value of 1.96 at the .05 level.

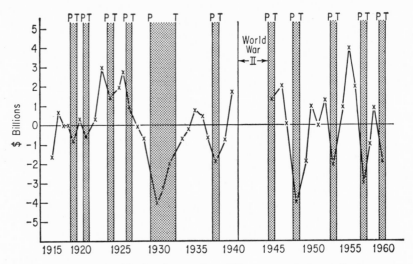

Chart V. Residuals of equation (29) compared to cyclical reference dates of N.B.E.R. P = peak, T = Trough (shaded areas represent periods of depressed economic activity)

Positive residuals indicate above-average investment expenditures, and low unemployment rates generally coincide with high levels of aggregate economic activity. We expect, therefore, that the regression coefficient for this test will be negative. The results are:

$$(32) \qquad u_t^{29} = +.820 - .108N_t^u,$$

"t" value $\qquad\qquad (2.52)$

$$\bar{r}^2 = .120, \qquad d = 1.34.$$

Hence, periods in which investment is relatively low are also characterized by high rates of unemployment.

Thus, the results of both of these tests lead us to conclude that the residuals of the model are significantly related to a measure of changes in the general level of economic activity. For forecasting purposes, however, we must be able to predict these changes in advance.

One operationally defined measure of these changes is a diffusion index of leading economic indicators, compiled by the National Bureau of Economic Research,[50] D_t^f. A test of the power of such a diffusion index

---

[50] Cf. *Business Cycle Indicators*, G. H. Moore, ed., National Bureau of Economic Research, Princeton University Press, Princeton, N. J., 1961 (2 vols.), and *Business Cycle Developments*, a monthly publication of the Department of Commerce.

to explain the residuals of equation (29) was made by regressing these residuals on the average value of the diffusion index for the last six months of the preceding year:

(33) $$u_t^{29} = 1.902 + .0348D'_t,$$
"t" value $\qquad$ (3.70)

$$\bar{R}^2 = .236, \qquad d = 1.48.$$

One fourth of the residual variance is explained by movements in predetermined values of the diffusion index of leading indicators. Thus, general cyclical movements appear to affect investment expenditures over and beyond that given by our original model.

Combining the results of (33) and (29) by including D'_t as an added independent variable in (29), we obtain

(34) $$I_t = -4.683 + .0318W_t + .657[\rho(.190) - r]_t$$
"t" values $\qquad$ (4.17) $\qquad$ (4.57)

$$+ .580I_{t-1} + .0437D'_t,$$
$$(4.36) \qquad (4.36)$$

$$\bar{R}^2 = .972, \qquad d = 1.70.$$

This equation is graphed by component in Chart VI.

Thus, by adding the last two variables, and, thereby, taking the effects of short-term factors into account, the fit of our model jumps from $\bar{R}^2 = .947$ in equation (15) to $\bar{R}^2 = .972$ in (34). The explanatory power of this expanded model appears quite satisfactory.[51]

Also, by adding these short-term considerations to our long-term explanation, we have virtually eliminated the serial correlation in our residuals. The critical value of d at the 5% level for 42 observations and 4 independent variables is 1.72, beyond which no significant evidence of positive serial correlation is indicated. The test value of our statistic ($= 1.70$) is obviously extremely close to this level.[52]

---

[51] Using the values of $\bar{R}^2$ from equations (29) and (34), we find that the partial correlation of D'_t with respect to I_t, given the prior effect of W_t, $[\rho(\eta) - r]_t$, and I_{t-1}, is .565. By Fisher's u-test, this is significant beyond the .001 level.

[52] Another test for the presence of serial correlation, the Von Neumann ratio, indicates that there is no evidence for the presence of serial correlation. The test value of the ratio is 1.74, while the critical value of the statistic, at the 5% level, is 1.54 with 42 observations.

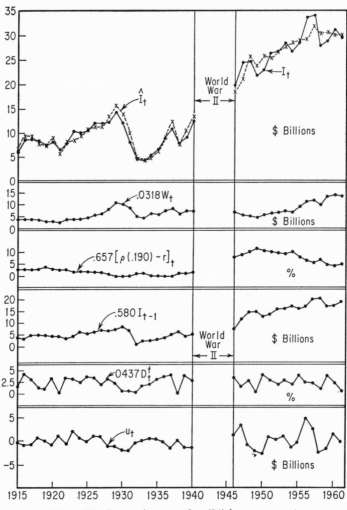

Chart VI. Regression equation (34) by component

D. Forecasting Investment Expenditures

As discussed in the opening pages of this study, one of the important reasons that investigation of the determinants of the volume of business investment expenditures is a worthwhile endeavor is that they play a critical role in stimulating and exacerbating changes in general economic activity. If undesired fluctuations in investment can be anticipated, presumably policies can be initiated either to forestall these changes or to counteract their effects by altering activity in some other sector of the system. While it has been the primary intention of the present study to identify and explore some basic long-term determinants of business investment, it is useful to scrutinize the model further by examining its predictive ability during recent years.

Of course, accurate forecasting over short periods of time is very dependent on efficient assimilation and interpretation of current data and conditions. The essential considerations underlying our model are those which center on long-term determinants of investment; the rather crude attempts to introduce short-term elements into our model in the preceding section cannot be expected to capture fully the effect of these fundamentally transitory factors. Nevertheless, we expect that predictions based on the model will approximate the magnitudes actually realized—for two reasons: (a) long-term determinants should exert a large enough impact to make themselves felt in periods of a year, and (b) statistically, the model has explained most of the variance in the investment series, indicating that short-term effects have been substantially incorporated.

In order that we might have some standards of comparison against which to judge the predictive value of our model, it was decided also to investigate the ability of four other methods of forecasting considered useful for this purpose. The forecasting models investigated are as follows:

(1) *The Adjusted Wealth Model.* The first method employs the model of the present study, the wealth model adjusted for short-term considerations. This is the model underlying equation (34) above.

(2) *McGraw-Hill Surveys of Business Plans.* Surveys of business intentions to invest have had an enviable record of forecasting aggregate investment expenditures during the postwar period. This is particularly so for those carried out by the Department of Commerce and the Securities and Exchange Commission. The forecasting abilities of these surveys have been subjected to several analyses in the past.[53] However, the Commerce–SEC survey is conducted in late January and February of the year for which the forecast is to be made, and the

---

[53] E.g., A. M. Okun, "The Predictive Value of Surveys of Business Intentions," *American Economic Review,* Papers and Proceedings, 1962, pp. 218–225, and "The Value of Anticipations Data in Forecasting National Product," pp. 407–451 in *The Quality and Economic Significance of Anticipations Data,* N.B.E.R., Princeton University Press, Princeton, N. J., 1960.

results become available only in early March—too late to be of assistance for a true forecast which is to be made at the beginning of the year.

The results of the McGraw-Hill surveys of business plans for investment in new plant and equipment are also made available after the year is under way, although somewhat earlier than those of the Commerce–SEC study. Thus, although forecasts taken from either of these sources will have a positive bias relative to any method which uses solely predetermined data (i.e., that which is available before the year begins), this bias is thought to be less for the McGraw-Hill surveys than for those of Commerce–SEC. Accordingly, the McGraw-Hill data are used as the second method of forecasting investment expenditures.

(3) *The Klein-Goldberger Model*. As discussed in Chapter 2, "profits" models of investment—in which measures of lagged or current profits and liquidity stock variables are used as the primary forces motivating investment expenditures—have been frequently advanced in the literature. One such model was included as a forecasting alternative.

The investment relation used for this purpose was that of the Klein–Goldberger (K–G) multi-equation econometric model of the United States.[54] The equation which results from their theoretical discussion relates investment to four independent variables: gross operating income, interest rates, the capital stock, and the stock of liquid assets. Empirical tests of their model revealed that interest rates, in marked contrast to their importance in our model, played a totally insignificant role. K–G dropped interest rates from further consideration.

The measure of investment used in the tests of the K–G model is much more aggregative than that in which we are interested. There, gross investment expenditures consisted of business' aggregate investment in plant and equipment plus aggregate investment in inventories and in residential construction. Nonetheless, the theoretical discussion which accompanies their formulation of the investment relation shows that investment by business in fixed capital comprises the basic motivation for their equation. Thus, if we eliminate residential construction and inventory investment, the explanatory power of their model should be increased.

---

[54] L. R. Klein and A. S. Goldberger, *An Econometric Model of the United States, 1929–1952*, North-Holland Publishing Company, Amsterdam, 1955. This model includes 14 endogenous variables. Four identities are included with ten structural equations. It is used by the authors to forecast economic activity.

A test of the K–G model in the present context obtained the following results. The data covered the period 1929–1961. Following K–G, 1941–1945 were excluded and lagged values of the profits variable were used:

$$(35) \quad I_t = -3.406 + .452\pi_{t-1} + .00266K_t^G + .267L_t - 1.150r_t,$$

"t" values $\quad\quad\quad\quad (4.47) \quad\quad (0.14) \quad\quad\quad (3.88) \quad\quad\quad (1.43)$

$$\bar{R}^2 = .933, \quad\quad d = 1.50,$$

where

π_{t-1} = lagged gross operating income (the sum of pretax profits, inventory valuation, depreciation, and interest paid),

L_t = business' stock of liquid assets at the beginning of the year,

and I_t, r_t, and K_t^G are as above.[55]

Our test supports the results obtained by K–G. As in their findings, the coefficients of interest rates and capital are both nonsignificant statistically. Following K–G, we have then eliminated interest rates only, and re-estimated the regression equation:

$$(36) \quad I_t = -9.273 + .488\pi_{t-1} - .0136K_t^G + .341L_t,$$

"t" values $\quad\quad\quad\quad (4.88) \quad\quad (0.75) \quad\quad\quad (7.34)$

$$\bar{R}^2 = .930, \quad\quad d = 1.64.$$

Sequential tests of the variables in this equation are used in the forecasting analysis below.

(4) *Naive I.* The basic naive model, that investment in year t will be the same as in year $t - 1$ (i.e., $I_t = I_{t-1}$), is the fourth method used to forecast investment. We take this as the minimal standard which any seriously proposed forecasting model should be able to outperform.

(5) *Naive II.* As explained below, the forecasting comparisons were made both in constant and in current dollars. To allow for a trend factor in the current dollar series, the naive I model was modified. In

---

[55] Goldsmith's estimates of the capital stock are not used by K–G in their tests. However, their estimates assume, with Goldsmith, a linear depreciation rate. Thus, if the stock of residential housing and of inventories were excluded from their estimate, it and K–G would probably closely correspond.

naive II, next year's investment is taken as this year's plus an adjustment for trend. In current dollars, investment expenditures increased by approximately 5 per cent per year during the decade examined. Thus, the fifth forecasting method takes predictions from the equation $I_t = 1.05 I_{t-1}$. This model was not used for the constant dollar comparisons in that no strong trend characterized these data.

The predictive ability of the above methods is compared using constant and current dollars. It is worth noting that, in contrast to several other studies of this nature, the predictions made by the five methods employed were in all cases true forecasts.[56] The forecasts made from the results of regression equations (i.e., the wealth model and the K–G relation) were obtained by using the estimates of coefficients based on all data up to the year for which the forecast is desired and the values of the (predetermined) variables relevant to that year.[57] After the forecast was made, this year was then incorporated in the estimates of the coefficients to be used to forecast the succeeding year's expenditures, and the cycle was repeated. Thus, the predictions are based completely on information which would be available to a forecaster at the time a forecast is made.

The forecasting comparison in constant dollars is the more interesting of the two. Our aim is to predict the real volume of investment, not a measure which is affected by price changes. Thus, the investment variables in these comparisons are deflated by our index of the price of physical capital, P^K. The major deficiency of such deflators over long periods is that they make no allowance for long-term changes in productivity per unit (cf. section A6). Since this factor is not expected to be overly important in a ten-year period, p^k was used because of its specific applicability to investment expenditures. The other variables in the equations tested[58] were deflated by the broadly based price index of privately produced gross national product.

The comparisons using current dollar valuations were made for two reasons. *First,* in the case of the anticipations data, one piece of available evidence indicates that many firms reporting to the Com-

---

[56] This excludes, of course, the bias incorporated in the anticipations data. In the wealth model, the interest rate observation used is that which prevailed during December of the preceding year. Thus, all "explanatory" variables used in forecasting from the wealth model are available on a predetermined basis.

[57] For the wealth model, that value of η was again chosen which maximized the fit of the model to the previous data.

[58] I.e., W_t in the wealth model; L_t, π_{t-1}, and K_t^g in the K–G relation.

merce-SEC survey already take price changes into account when reporting investment intentions.[59] Thus, the McGraw-Hill data may be similarly affected. *Second*, price deflators are not infallible, and it is possible that they introduce more bias than they eliminate. Indeed, similar studies made previously by both Okun and members of the McGraw-Hill Department of Economics[60] do not even comment on this point but proceed directly in terms of current dollars.

Four summary measures of performance of the forecasting methods discussed above are given: (a) median absolute percentage error (Md), (b) mean absolute percentage error (Mn), (c) root-mean-square percentage error (RMS), and (d) mean percentage error. The first two of these were calculated to measure the average forecasting error over the period. Since extreme errors in only one or two years will tend to have large effects on the mean value of the sample as a whole, the median measure was also included. The root-mean-square percentage error was added in an effort to gain some notion of the dispersion of forecasting error over the decade tested. The mean percentage error can be used as an average estimate of the forecasting bias of the various methods, since in its compilation positive and negative errors cancel.

The results of this experiment are given in Tables 2 and 3 in constant and current dollars, respectively. The performances of the forecasting methods according to the four criteria are ranked on the left-hand side of these tables. The forecasts made by the various methods are shown graphically in Charts VII and VIII.

The results indicate that the forecasting record of the wealth model is, on the whole, quite good. In the constant dollar comparisons of Table 2, it is ranked first on all four criteria. Its average error of forecast, as indicated by both the Md and Mn absolute percentage measures, is substantially better than that of the McGraw-Hill surveys, enjoying an advantage of over 1 per cent according to these criteria.[61] The K–G relation is disappointing. Even the naive model does better by all but the RMS criteria. Moreover, like the McGraw-Hill surveys, the K–G relation overestimates investment expenditures quite consistently.

---

[59] *Survey of Current Business*, March 1956, p. 20.

[60] Okun, cf. footnote 53, and D. M. Keezer, R. P. Ulin, D. Greenwald, and M. Matulis, "Observations on the Predictive Quality of McGraw-Hill Surveys of Business' Plans for New Plants and Equipment," pp. 369–385 in *The Quality and Economic Significance of Anticipations Data, op. cit.*

[61] An error of 1 per cent implies, on average over the decade, an error of $.29 billion in constant 1954 dollars.

Turning to the current dollar comparisons of Table 3, we find that the wealth model again does reasonably well. It is ranked second according to the first three criteria, and first according to the last measure. The McGraw-Hill surveys rank first in Mn and RMS, but the bias imparted in their favor due to the late date at which they are collected may account for their slight edge along these criteria (i.e., less than one percentage point in both cases[62]). The K–G relation is outperformed again by the basic naive model when Md is used as the criterion. Naive II does surprisingly well during six of the ten years, but, obviously, its inability to forecast the important turning points leads it into making some very large errors. These are indicated by the RMS criterion. It is ranked last by this measure.

As expected, the basic naive forecast has, in general, low relative rankings in both the constant and current dollar comparisons. Both the causal models and the survey data are in fact helpful when making forecasts. Since these models are designed to reflect basic underlying determinants of investment and/or short-term considerations affecting investment decisions in any given year, this is encouraging.

In both Tables 2 and 3, all the models ran into at least two years when they misforecasted investment expenditures by 10 per cent or more, a sizable margin of error. In particular, the substantial drop in investment from 1957 to 1958 was underestimated by all the models, and all but the K–G relation had great difficulty in predicting during the boom of 1956.

Of the forecasting methods investigated, the least biased, as indicated by mean percentage error, is the wealth model in both constant and current dollar analyses. Of course, this is not an unmixed blessing. If a method gives forecasts which are consistently biased in the same direction, a correction factor can be introduced which will, on average, improve its forecasts. The only method of those examined here which possesses such a persistent bias is the McGraw-Hill surveys. During the decade investigated, the estimates obtained from this source consistently overstated actual expenditures. However, these surveys have been conducted since 1948, and the forecasts they imply for the three years preceding 1952 understated actual expenditures by 14 per cent in 1948, 4 per cent in 1949, and 20 per cent in 1950. Any correction for bias with this history in mind would have to be made quite cautiously.

---

[62] An error of 1 per cent implies an average current dollar misforecast of $.32 billion over the decade 1952–1961.

Thus, we have found that our model fares well, on the basis of selected criteria, when compared to certain other models in forecasting investment. Abstracting from price changes, the model outperformed the other alternatives analyzed. When using current dollar valuations, the McGraw-Hill surveys, in general, outperform our model, although both their late availability and the consistent bias in their estimates militate against their sole use in any forecasting scheme. The additional information provided by our model—both quantitatively and qualitatively—may aid economic forecasters of the future.

E. Summary

In this chapter, we have subjected the investment equation, which resulted from the theoretical model of the firm presented in Chapter 3, to a number of empirical tests. These tests were made at an aggregative level and included all private nonagricultural investment in plant and equipment. We have found that the model explains the data quite well.

A specific test for the significance of interest rates in the investment relation indicated that they do indeed play an important role in explaining the volume of investment expenditures. This contrasts the results of prior investigations made by other researchers. We interpreted this as supporting both the theory presented earlier and our contention, made in Chapter 2, that the eclectic approach used in many earlier studies has resulted in mis-specification of the theoretical notions to be tested. This has led to erroneous conclusions—in this case about the role of interest rates. Further discussion of the specific effects on investment caused by variations in interest rates is included in the next chapter.

We have also found that the investment relation implied by our model has apparently been stable over time. This stability was seen to include the years of the Great Depression, which led to the conclusion that one need not invoke arguments involving the structural collapse of the economic system to explain the low levels of investment by private business which occurred during that period. It was pointed out, however, that no such statement can be made about the stability of other sectors of the economy based only on this evidence, and that such arguments might still have their place in explaining the movements of the causal variables contained in our investment relation.

Short-term factors were introduced into the model. It was found that both the effect of the incompleted plans of past years and the current level of activity in other sectors of the economy help to explain

the current level of investment expenditures during the period investigated. For prediction purposes it is necessary, when using a single equation, that all independent variables be predetermined. Thus, the lagged
value of a diffusion index of leading indicators was used as a surrogate
for a measure of current levels of general business activity and was
found to enter significantly into the regression equation.

Finally, the ability of the model to predict investment expenditures
during the decade beginning in 1952 was compared to other forecasting
methods. Our model was seen to perform quite respectably when judged
both by four forecasting criteria and on its performance relative to
those of the other methods.

Thus, on the basis of the empirical tests that have been performed
in this chapter, we conclude that the theory of the firm presented in
Chapter 3 does adequately represent important economic processes
which underlie the decision to invest in physical capital. The pertinence
of our model to the mainstream of economic theory, its implications for
policy considerations, and its relationship to alternative models of the
investment decision have not yet been fully established. Accordingly,
attention will be turned to these tasks in the concluding chapter, which
follows.

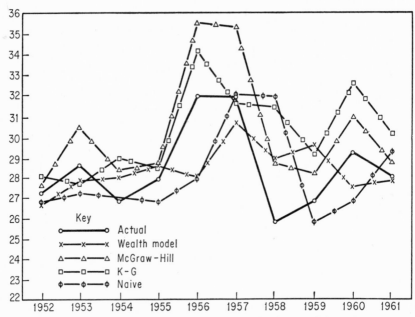

Chart VII. Data of Table II. Forecasts by four models 1952–
1961 constant dollars (1954 = 100)

TABLE 2. COMPARISON OF FOUR METHODS OF FORECASTING BUSINESS' INVESTMENT DURING THE DECADE 1952–1961
[constant dollars (1954 = 100)]

Year:	1952	1953	1954	1955	1956	1957	1958	1959	1960	1961	Summary Measurement of Performance[4]			
											Md Abs. % = rank	Mn Abs. % = rank	RMS = rank	Mn % = rank
Actual:[1]	27.26	28.61	26.83	27.92	32.01	31.95	25.78	26.85	29.25	27.99				
Method[2]														
1 (Wealth)	26.66	27.85	28.00	28.59	27.98	30.71	28.95	29.58	27.54	27.87	4.12 = 1	5.69 = 1	7.04 = 1	.27 = 1
% err.[3]	−2.19	−2.67	4.36	2.40	−12.59	−3.88	12.35	10.18	−5.84	−.44				
2 (McGraw-Hill)	27.57[5]	30.51[5]	28.39[5]	28.69	35.56	35.42	28.72	28.22	31.04	28.79	6.38 = 3	6.75 = 2	7.63 = 2	6.75 = 4
% err.	1.44	6.64	5.81	2.76	11.09	10.86	11.40	8.83	6.12	2.86				
3 (K-G)	28.11	27.69	29.04	28.44	34.20	31.66	31.45	29.11	32.58	30.09	7.19 = 4	7.13 = 4	9.33 = 3	6.53 = 3
% err.	3.15	−.92	8.23	1.86	6.86	−.91	21.99	8.43	11.39	7.52				
4 (Naive I)	26.82	27.26	28.61	26.83	27.92	32.01	31.95	25.78	26.85	29.25	4.39 = 2	6.98 = 3	9.59 = 4	.35 = 2
% err.	−1.61	−4.22	6.63	−3.90	−12.78	.02	23.93	−3.99	−8.21	4.50				

(Notes on pages 97, 98)

TABLE 3. COMPARISON OF FIVE METHODS OF FORECASTING BUSINESS' INVESTMENT DURING THE DECADE 1952–1961

(current dollars)

Year:	1952	1953	1954	1955	1956	1957	1958	1959	1960	1961	Summary Measures of Performance[4]			
											Md Abs. % = rank	Mn Abs. % = rank	RMS % = rank	Mn % = rank
Actual:[1]	26.49	28.32	26.83	28.70	35.08	36.96	30.53	32.54	35.68	34.37				
Method:[2]														
1 (Wealth)	25.35	27.02	28.29	29.14	30.70	35.20	35.02	36.37	36.54	36.90				
% err.[3]	−4.31	−4.59	5.44	1.54	−12.50	−4.77	14.71	11.78	2.41	7.37	5.10 = 2	6.58 = 2	8.09 = 2	1.67 = 1
2 (McGraw-Hill)	26.80[5]	30.02[5]	28.39[5]	29.49	38.97	40.98	34.01	34.21	37.87	35.35				
% err.	1.14	5.97	5.83	2.74	11.07	10.87	11.42	5.12	6.14	2.85	5.90 = 3	6.32 = 1	7.29 = 1	6.32 = 5
3 (K-G)	28.55	28.45	29.87	29.46	33.20	33.73	37.04	35.56	38.48	36.54				
% err.	7.75	.45	1.35	2.64	−5.07	−8.74	21.34	9.26	7.84	6.32	7.80 = 5	8.08 = 4	9.70 = 3	5.32 = 4
4 (Naive I)	25.64	26.49	28.32	26.83	28.70	35.08	36.96	30.53	32.54	35.68				
% err.	−3.20	−6.46	5.57	−6.53	−18.19	−5.09	21.08	−6.20	−8.79	3.81	6.37 = 4	8.49 = 5	10.28 = 4	−2.40 = 2
5 (Naive II)	26.93	27.82	29.74	28.17	30.14	36.84	38.81	32.05	34.17	37.46				
% err.	1.63	1.78	10.85	−1.86	−13.81	−.34	27.13	−1.51	−4.23	8.99	3.05 = 1	7.21 = 3	10.95 = 5	2.51 = 3

(Notes on pages 97, 98)

NOTES

TABLES 2 AND 3

1. Source: Department of Commerce-Securities and Exchange Commission series on expenditures on new plant and equipment by U.S. business. In Table 1, this series is deflated by the price index for physical capital, P^K.

2. The methods are as follows:

1. Wealth model adjusted for short-term considerations, employing the variables underlying equation (34) of the text.

2. McGraw-Hill surveys of business' plans for new plants and equipment (source: annual reports of the McGraw-Hill Publishing Company).

3. Klein-Goldberger investment relation, employing the variables underlying equation (36) of the test.

4. Naive model, $I_t = I_{t-1}$.

5. For current dollar comparisons only (i.e., Table 3), the naive model adjusted for trend, $I_t = 1.05I_{t-1}$.

The investment variables in these equations were deflated by P^K and the non-investment variables (i.e., those measured in terms of dollars) were deflated by the index of prices for privately produced gross national product when making the constant dollar comparisons in Table 2.

3. Percentage error is calculated as:

$$\% \text{ err.} = 100(\text{predicted} - \text{actual})/\text{actual}.$$

4. The four summary measures of performance over the decade are as follows:

Md Abs. % = Median absolute percentage error, computed as the mid-point of the fifth and sixth largest absolute errors of forecast;

Mn Abs. % = Mean absolute percentage error, computed as the sum of the ten absolute percentage errors divided by ten;

RMS = Root-mean-square error of forecast, computed as the square root of the sum of the squared percentage errors of forecast divided by ten;

Mn % = Mean percentage error, computed as the sum of the percentage errors divided by ten.

The performances of the forecasting methods are ranked on the basis of these measures. This ranking is indicated by the number following the " = " sign after the measure. The closer is the measure to zero (i.e., perfect forecast), the better is the performance and the higher is the ranking. A rank of "1" indicates best performance of the alternatives along this criterion, "2" indicates second best, etc.

5. For the years preceding 1955, the McGraw-Hill survey data were not gathered for the commercial sector of private business. Thus, the forecasts given in Tables 2 and 3 for the McGraw-Hill surveys before 1955 assume that their error of forecast on the commercial sector, which they did not include, would have been equal to that of all the remaining sectors, which they do include. After 1955, the McGraw-Hill data are exactly comparable to the Commerce-SEC series.

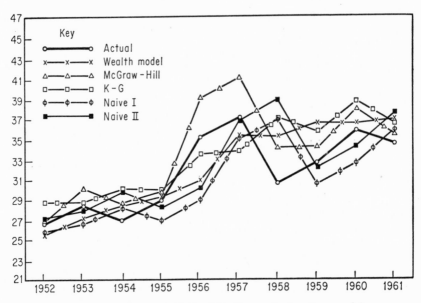

Chart VIII. Data of Table III. Forecasts by five models 1952–1961 current dollars

CHAPTER 5

Synopsis and Implications

The investment equation tested in the preceding chapter is the direct outgrowth of the model of the firm presented in Chapter 3. As such it differs markedly from those tested by many of the previous investigators discussed in Chapter 3. As there indicated, the usual approach in empirical work has been to select several variables which are thought to be related to investment expenditures, and then attempt to establish a statistical relationship between them. The selection of variables is made without benefit of any explicit theoretical model of the process being tested. Two important weaknesses ensue from this procedure.

The *first* of these concerns the specifics of the empirical work itself. With no underlying explicit theoretical foundation, it is impossible to avoid arbitrary specifications of the functional form of the equation tested and the form in which the various selected variables enter this equation. Since no framework has been established, the implications of the assumptions cannot be pursued.[1] Thus, it is difficult to place con-

---

[1] In the present model the assumption that the desired stock of assets is a linear function of W, ρ_a, and ρ_l, was found to imply linear approximations to the curves relating return on assets (liabilities) to the quantity of assets (liabilities) (cf. footnote 25, Chapter 3). It is impossible to similarly trace Klein's asumption that his investment equation is a linear function of the variables he employs. Also, while net revenues are found to enter our investment equation in the form of yields, no such justification exists for Klein's use of absolute profits in his equation (Klein, *op. cit.*, 1950). The kind of information which is obtainable from explicit mathematical development of the model from which the investment equation is derived *cannot* be secured from essentially literary discussion disguised as mathematics with the use of symbols and arrows (e.g., R. Eisner, "A Distributed Lag Investment Function," *Econometrica*, 1960).

fidence in the equation utilized or to assign explicit meaning to the results.

The *second* weakness of previous empirical research concerns its larger role as a contribution to economic theory which advances the economist's view and understanding of the world. Since the assumptions employed are difficult to identify, lack of theoretical groundwork severely hinders the interpretation which is to be given the results.[2] Yet, the ultimate significance of economic research resides in its interpretation.

The results of the present study are especially interesting in that they support the portfolio-balance model of Chapter 3, from which the investment equation tested is explicitly derived. These results have important theoretical consequences, and it is to these that the present chapter is devoted.

This chapter is divided into four parts. In Part A, the reasoning which underlies the theoretical development of Chapter 3 is briefly reviewed along with the evidence which was adduced in support of the model. Implications of our results for some of the theoretical questions raised earlier (in Chapter 2) are discussed. Some limitations of the model and several lines along which our approach can be extended in future research are noted. Part B investigates some implications of the portfolio-balance model and the importance of including stocks and relative yields in models of economic processes. Policy implications are examined in Part C. The chapter concludes with a summary section which relates our results to the broader questions raised in the opening chapter.

A. The Model and Evidence: Brief Review

The motivational assumption upon which the model is founded is that the firm behaves so as to achieve an optimal portfolio of assets and liabilities. It is in the search for profits that decisions are made to alter the firm's portfolio position. Thus, it is the profit equation which serves as the criterion function.

Investment expenditures are viewed as the result of decisions made to adjust the stock of (physical) capital to some desired level. To understand the considerations underlying these decisions, attention must be

---

[2] The lack of theoretical structure in Grunfeld's study, for example, leads to one result which he is at a loss to explain, but which is easily interpreted within the framework of the present model. Cf. section A1, below.

focused first on the desired demand for stocks themselves. The model defines profits as the difference between the return from the stock of assets and the stream of liabilities held by the firm. Given the relationships between these stocks and the flows which they produce, the decision problem of the firm is to adjust its portfolio optimally.

The cost of liabilities (i.e., the interest rate) is taken as an increasing function of the firm's debt-equity ratio, and the marginal yield on assets is taken as a nonincreasing function of the stock of assets, an implication shown to result from horizontal or downward-sloping demand curves in the market in which the firm sells its output. The constraint within which portfolio adjustment decisions are assumed to be made is that the wealth (equity) of the firm is determined by the market value of the original portfolio. Thus, it is wealth which imposes an ultimate limit on size, since growth beyond the point where marginal returns and payments are equal will be unprofitable and, therefore, avoided by the firm.

Solving the equations analytically, we find the desired stock of assets to be a function of wealth, the rate of return on assets, and the rate of payment required by creditors. In the case of physical assets, instantaneous adjustment of actual to desired stocks is generally unlikely owing to the inevitable delays caused by such things as construction and planning lags. Thus, investment was taken as proportional to the difference between the firm's actual stock of assets and the desired level. When aggregated and put into a form suitable for statistical test, the investment function was found to be increasing with respect to wealth and expected yields and decreasing with respect to interest rates and the present capital stock.

Because of statistical difficulties in distinguishing between wealth and capital, a modified version of the model was used in the bulk of the statistical tests. The data used were aggregate investment expenditures of private nonagricultural business from 1915–1961, excluding the years of World War II. The model fitted the data quite closely. It exhibited functional stability over time. When adjusted for essentially short-term aberrations, its predictive ability was respectable. All parameters were statistically significant and of the expected signs. A stringent requirement of the underlying theory—that the parameters of yields and interest costs be of the same magnitude but of the opposite sign—was confirmed by the data. The optimal value of an externally specified coefficient of expectations was remarkedly stable throughout. Thus, the results of the tests provide a substantial foundation for the model.

A1. Some Earlier Questions. The theory and evidence for the investment relation of the present study provide us with insights into some questions about previous research raised in Chapter 2. *First,* our model makes explicit the rationale behind the "residual funds" hypothesis in which the stock of liquid assets is taken as a determinant of investment. The stocks of liquid assets are highly correlated with measures of wealth,[3] which suggests that these liquidity stocks are surrogates for the wealth variable in the investment equation. Indeed, to repeat our previous position, we cannot believe that investment decisions are made without regard to the conditions of external financing. The major premise of the residual funds hypothesis is that entrepreneurs will tend to shy away from investment outlays which must be financed by resort to external funds. But surely it is the cost of funds, not their origin, which is the deciding factor in the determination of whether or not a given investment program should be undertaken.[4]

Second, our model also explains why, in many previous empirical inquiries, measures of the capital stock entered the investment function with positive regression coefficients, contrary to the expectations of the investigators. Since wealth and capital are highly correlated, capital also serves as a surrogate for wealth. Our model implies, and the data suggest, that wealth is positively related to investment. Thus, the model explains a result which previous investigators have found difficult to interpret.

Third, the present model indicates that both yields and interest costs play an important role in the investment equation. At a stipulated point in time, wealth is given. Investment, or an expansion in assets, can occur only with a corresponding increase in liabilities. The model and empirical tests suggest that it is yield *relative* to the costs of liability expansion, which is the critical determinant of investment expenditures, not absolute profits alone, as has been often suggested in the past.

---

[3] For example, the simple correlation between the stock of liquid assets used in the K–G relation of Chapter 4 and the market value of equities, using the current dollar figures at the beginning of the year, 1929–1940; 1946–1961, is .74.

[4] Cf., e.g., the corroborating evidence presented by J. Lintner, in E. S. Mason, *The Corporation in Modern Society, op. cit.* Internal liquidity may be of importance in certain short-run situations, especially in the case of smaller, marginal firms whose access to capital markets is decidedly limited. Even here, however, we would expect that funds would be forthcoming from external sources if the proposed venture is potentially profitable. Of course, since these smaller firms make only small contributions to the aggregate level of investment expenditures, this argument for internal liquidity may not be of any importance when seeking determinants of total investment,

Thus, our results confirm the position of several recent investigations which argue against the importance of absolute profits as a determinant of investment expenditures.[5]

Finally, the model proposed by Grunfeld also fits into our framework. His market value variable is closely allied to the measure of wealth utilized in the preceding chapter. In addition, our framework helps explain a puzzle raised by Grunfeld's results, which he was not able to solve,[6] i.e., that the estimated coefficient for the capital stock was much higher than expected. After suggesting some possible explanations, Grunfeld concludes his section as follows:

> This fact casts some doubt on the adequacy of our model to explain investment expenditures. Some important effect of size on the decision to invest may exist which has not been incorporated formally into the investment model constructed ....[7]

From the perspective of the model developed here, it appears that the missing effect to which Grunfeld alludes is provided by the explicit incorporation of wealth as a determinant of investment expenditures.

A2. Qualifications and Possible Extensions. Before turning to the theoretical and policy implications of the model, it is helpful first to review its major shortcomings. We regard the present study as including three important weaknesses to which the efforts of future research might be profitably directed.

First, the present model was constructed in a static environment and, as such, the effects of changing relationships between variables were not explicitly incorporated into the decision framework. One result of this treatment of time is that all new financing had to be considered as emanating from the issuing of liabilities, i.e., the amount of equity was taken as nonalterable at the moment the investment decision was made. Dynamic elements introduced into the model will appreciably extend its generality.

Second, the theoretical development was done in the context of one homogeneous asset and one homogeneous liability. The complications which result from interactions between different assets and liabilities were thereby avoided. An extension of the model which includes various categories of assets and liabilities will be needed, especially in the attempt

---

[5] Cf. Grunfeld and the studies by Eisner, cited above.

[6] Grunfeld, *op. cit.*, pp. 255–257.

[7] *Ibid.*, p. 257.

to explain concurrent changes in various macroeconomic variables.[8] Tests of this extended model will involve simultaneous consideration of changes in each separate category introduced, and will require investigations which go far beyond the determinants of physical investment alone. Present tests were made in a single equation structure, following the general pattern of empirical testing in the investment literature. This approach involves the assumption that all the explanatory variables[9] are predetermined constants. In fact, these quantities are economic variables of importance in their own right in the larger system and are no doubt affected to some extent by the same influences which affect our measures of investment. Thus, a more complete, multi-equation structural model may lead to further implications of the present model.[10]

Third, we have been subject to the usual inability to acquire dependable measures of the relevant variables in our investment equation. Our measure of expectations, though widely used, is derived from past data, no estimates of future activity entering.[11] It is hoped that present work being done in the area of business anticipations might be helpful in ameliorating this deficiency. We also confronted the measurement problem when dealing with the capital stock and wealth variables, as discussed in the preceding chapter.

Possibly one other primary criticism can be directed to the aggregative nature of the tests. It may well be that microeconomic studies will

---

[8] A model incorporating two assets is presented by J. Tobin, "A Dynamic Aggregative Model," *Journal of Political Economy*, 1955, pp. 103–115. An extended version of this model is discussed by Tobin in "Money, Capital, and Other Stores of Value," *Proceedings of the American Economic Association*, 1961, pp. 26–37. A general equilibrium stock-flow model is presented by A. H. Meltzer, and K. Brunner, "The Place of Financial Intermediaries in the Transmission of Monetary Policy," *American Economic Review*, May 1963.

[9] I.e., the independent variables of the regression equation.

[10] Other structural candidates for a model whose equations would reflect emphasis on wealth are readily suggested. Meltzer, in "The Demand for Money: The Evidence from the Time Series," *Journal of Political Economy*, forthcoming, has shown that the demand for money is explainable from an equation using wealth and interest rates as principal independent variables. Similarly, recent work on the consumption function has also been derived from a framework substantially similar to a wealth model. E.g., F. Modigliani and R. Brumberg, "Utility Analysis and the Consumption Function," in *Post-Keynesian Economics*, K. Kurihara, ed., and M. Friedman, *A Theory of the Consumption Function*, National Bureau of Economic Research, New York, 1957.

[11] The extent to which this approach has been used in estimating expectations by other investigators is indicated in footnote 3, Chapter 4. This approach is not accepted by all researchers, however. See, e.g., J. F. Muth, "Rational Expectations and the Theory of Price Movements," *Econometrica*, 1961, pp. 315–335.

provide evidence that is not entirely consistent with our results. However, as stated at the outset of the study, our concern is with aggregate activity. Our efforts have not been directed toward formulating an accurate description of the process by which investment decisions of a given firm are made. Although it is certain that decisions of individual economic units might on occasion be motivated by forces other than those which we have examined, the decision processes and the parameter estimates in which we are interested are those which reflect the reactions of the aggregate economic community. The success of the model in this respect, as reported in Chapter 4, leads us to believe that further work, especially along the lines indicated above, will be fruitful.

B. Theoretical Implications of the Model

As discussed in Chapter 2, many recent models of investment behavior are based on various modifications of the accelerator model, in which changes in flows (profits or output) are taken to be the primary determinants of investment activity. We have not used this framework. Instead, we have utilized a portfolio-balance theory in which investment was found to be the result of a process of adjusting actual stocks of physical capital to desired levels. We shall now discuss the theoretical implications of our approach, compare it to the implications of the widely accepted accelerator model, and briefly explore its relationship to other theories of macroeconomic activity.

B1. Portfolio-balance Approach. In Chapter 3, a model was developed which views the investment decision as emanating from a desire of the firm to optimize its balance sheet position, a procedure which was found to depend on the relative yields of the portfolio components. The decision to invest in one asset, physical capital, cannot be made independently of decisions concerning the other elements of the portfolio.

Thus, our work is similar in spirit to, and supports the insights of, Friedman, Tobin, and Brunner, among others.[12] They argue that since

---

[12] Tobin, *op. cit.*; M. Friedman, "The Quality Theory of Money—A Restatement," Chapter 1 in *Studies in the Quality Theory of Money*, M. Friedman, ed., University of Chicago Press, Chicago, 1956; K. Brunner, "The Report of the Commission on Money and Credit," *Journal of Political Economy*, 1961, pp. 605–620. R. Turvey has also supported this approach. See his *Interest Rates and Asset Prices*, The Macmillan Company, London, 1961.

it is the changes in demand for stocks of assets that give rise to the flows (e.g., investment) with which we are concerned, it is necessary to concentrate primary attention directly on the variables of central interest, *viz.*, relative yields, on which desired stocks depend. Attention is thus taken from flows alone and refocused on the more basic stock-flow relationships.

Concern with desired stocks of assets has been most common in work done on the demand for money.[13] Since households and business firms can adjust their cash balances quickly to changes in economic conditions, it is assumed that actual money balances closely approximate desired balances. Effort is then focused on specifying the variables on which the desired balances depend and testing the relationship posited.

One of the major characteristics of physical capital which distinguishes it from money or bonds is that it takes time t adjust the stock of capital from one level to another. While the portfolio-balance approach has been shown to be applicable to the demand for money, it might appear questionable that its propositions would be as helpful when dealing with an asset for which the desired stock can never be directly measured because of the long period of adjustment required.

Hence, a primary conclusion of the present study is that it is indeed useful to view the demand for capital, at least in the aggregate, through the perspectives provided by portfolio-balance theory. Even though the desired stock of capital can never be isolated, it is nonetheless fruitful to view investment decisions as part of the broader framework in which assets are allocated as functions of their relative costs and yields.

B2. Comparison with Accelerator Theories. It is interesting to contrast the conclusion that assets are allocated according to their relative yields with the position implied by the accelerator theories. As indicated above, the accelerator models are formulated in terms of other flow variables such as output or profits. The models state that changes in these variables will induce changes in investment activity. The yields which can be earned by holding assets other than real capital are thus irrelevant to these models. In particular, on the basis of empirical tests made via the accelerator models, the conclusion emerges that interest rates are not pertinent in determining the level of investment expenditures.[14] Indeed, if the investment relation is insensitive to

---

[13] E.g., Cagan, "The Monetary Dynamics of Hyperinflation," Chapter 2 in *Studies in the Quantity Theory of Money, op. cit.*, and A. H. Meltzer, *op. cit.*

[14] Cf., e.g., R. Eisner, "Interview and Other Survey Techniques and the Study of Investment," pp. 503–584 in *Problems of Capital Formation*, National Bureau of Economic Research, New York 1957.

interest rates and the yields on other assets (i.e., substitutes for capital in a given portfolio), the incentive to invest must come through an accelerator or product demand mechanism.

However, the results of Chapter 4 strongly suggest that investment expenditures are *not* insensitive to interest rates and, thus, that it is the relative yield on real capital which is relevant to the determination of the desired stock of physical capital. When estimating both the basic, long-run investment function and the short-term equation (in which adjustments are made to account for the partially completed plans of earlier years) interest rates enter with statistically significant negative coefficients.[15]

This result has extreme significance in our efforts to understand the processes underlying changes in economic activity. The monetary authorities have the power to change the structure of relative yields by an open market operation, by changing the reserve requirements of commercial banks, or by modifying other policy variables under their control. They can thus alter the desired portfolios of economic units, which affect the tempo of economic activity by inducing portfolio adjustments. By identifying those yields and interactions which are relevant to changes in a given asset, it is possible to trace the movements in activity which are induced by changes in a given set of yields.

It is apparent that the conceptual framework supplied by portfolio-balance theory is of much wider applicability than the mechanistic principle of the accelerator. This is not to deny that the insights provided by this principle are sometimes useful. In the present model, the yield on assets is surely related to demand and productive capacity as suggested by the accelerator, and it is expected that the acceleration principle may prove useful in many short-term situations characterized by steadily increasing demand and relatively constant capital-output ratios. The basic point, however, is that capital investment may be, in general, more fruitfully viewed as an integral aspect of the asset allocation process rather than as a result of the application of essentially rigid rules which do not take into consideration the effects of changes in other sectors of the economic system. Such changes, while not immediately affecting output or profits, may very well result in changes in the structure of relative yields and thereby affect the volume of investment expenditures undertaken by economic units.[16]

---

[15] Equations (16) and (30), Chapter 4.

[16] This point is alluded to by F. Modigliani in his "Comment," pp. 450–463 in *Problems of Capital Formation, op. cit.*

B3. Macroeconomic Theories. One widely accepted model of macroeconomic activity is the income-expenditure model which was first presented by Keynes.[17] This theory assigns dominant roles to flow variables such as income, consumption, and investment. The model underlying the present study is presented in terms of stocks and relative yields. While changes in desired stocks give rise to the flows of the income-expenditure model, it is important to distinguish the role of stocks in the two theories.

In the income-expenditure model, the only stocks explicitly admitted into the model are the stocks of money and bonds.[18] Stocks of other variables are not considered. Attention is centered on the circular aspect of economic activity, illustrated by the truism that one person's expenditure is another's income. Some modifications have been introduced in an effort to circumvent the Pigou-Patinkin "real balance effect," which relates changes in the price level to changes in real wealth and thus to expenditures.[19] However, these have been essentially halfhearted and have tended to be concentrated in changes in the specification of the consumption function, so that wealth is now added to income as a causal variable underlying consumption expenditures.[20]

Stocks of assets thus play a fundamentally different role in the income-expenditure model as opposed to the portfolio-balance theory. In the former model, the stock of one asset (money) is singled out as of basic importance, and other stocks are virtually ignored except in periods of drastic changes in the price level. All primary flows are essentially taken as dependent on other flows only. Relative yields, which are taken as the basic activators of these flows in the portfolio-balance model, are largely disregarded. As in our discussion of the accelerator models above, this implies that changes in flows induced by alterations in the structure of relative yields will be overlooked. Thus, the income-expenditure model is an incomplete description of economic activity, since it ignores variables which we have found to be important determinants of investment activity.

---

[17] J. M. Keynes, *The General Theory of Employment, Interest and Money*, Harcourt, Brace & World, Inc., London, 1936.

[18] Keynes, of course, was primarily concerned with activity over short periods of time and, as such, assumed the capital stock to be constant at a given level.

[19] D. Patinkin, *Money, Interest and Prices*, Harper & Row, Publishers, New York, 1956; A. C. Pigou, "Economic Progress in a Stable Environment," *Economica*, 1947.

[20] Work on the consumption function by both Friedman (1957) and Modigliani and Brumberg, *op. cit.*, are illustrative of efforts to incorporate wealth into this equation, although neither has been presented as an attempt to bolster the income-expenditure approach.

An alternative theoretical framework of economic activity is provided by the quantity theory of money, in which interest has revived in recent years.[21] Like the portfolio-balance model, it views flows as resulting from decisions to alter asset portfolios. The two theories also coincide in their desire to find functional specifications of the demand for assets which exhibit stability over time. Such stability is necessary if we are to trace the effects of proposed policy decisions.

The theories differ in the emphasis on the importance of different assets. As summarized by Tobin,

> the modern quantity-of-money theorist[22] ... holds that virtually everything of strategic importance in the capital account can be studied by focusing on the supply and demand for money. This view ... has been persuasively opposed by Gurley and Shaw.[23] As they point out, it is not hard to describe events and policies that raise the supply price of capital[24] while leaving the quantity of money unchanged or even increasing it.[25]

The implication of this last statement is that, through the workings of financial intermediaries, the yield on capital relative to money might be changed even though the stocks of both assets remain constant. Thus, when we attempt to construct a framework through which the macroeconomic system can be perceived, it is abortive to concentrate attention on one asset at the expense of others. If we have learned anything from general-equilibrium theory, it is the fact that simultaneity must be a necessary element in the economist's view of the world. An expanded portfolio-balance model with supporting empirical evidence, in which the desired stocks of various critical assets and the flows to which they give rise are simultaneously determined, appears to provide the most promising approach to the framework desired.

---

[21] M. Friedman, (1956).

[22] To whom velocity is a stable function of identifiable variables, whereas his classical counterpart regarded velocity as a fixed constant.

[23] J. Gurley and E. S. Shaw, *Money in a Theory of Finance*, The Brookings Institution, Washington, D.C., 1960. In this book it is argued that since the liabilities issued by financial intermediaries are close substitutes for money, changes in the level of activity by these intermediaries can alter the yield on money even though the stock of money remains unchanged.

[24] I.e., the rate of return on capital demanded by wealthholders to absorb the existing capital stock into their portfolios.

[25] Tobin, 1961, pp. 35–36.

C. Policy Implications

One of the major reasons that we seek an explicit operational framework with which to view the workings of the economic system is that the propositions forthcoming from such a framework allow us to evaluate better the usefulness of various policy decisions, thereby promoting our ability to control and direct the economy. The specific empirical results of this study, and the wider theoretical apparatus of which the present model is a part, derive significance from their policy implications. These implications will now be briefly discussed.

As outlined previously, in many recent theories of investment expenditures (e.g., residual funds theories, accelerator models), relative yields have been relegated to an insignificant role. In particular, it is argued that interest rates are not critical determinants of investment, and that the interest elasticity of investment can be taken as zero, for all practical purposes. One implication of this position is that policy decisions designed to alter the structure of yields on assets will be largely irrelevant in determining the volume of investment activity which will be undertaken by a private business. Thus, the efforts of the monetary authorities to manipulate interest rates are destined to be ineffective as a means of influencing investment expenditures.[26]

Contrary to this position, portfolio-balance theory argues that changes in economic activity depend on the structure of relative yields. Thus, to the extent that monetary policy can affect the relative yield structure, it derives support from the theory *in spite of* our inability to detect empirically direct effects of interest rates on investment.

Nonetheless, this inability has been admittedly disconcerting to the proponents of monetary policy. On intuitive grounds alone, interest rates should represent one yield to which investment expenditures are closely related. However, most investigations into the empirical relationship between interest rates and investment have not lent credence to this position. Summary statements made by the authors of two large surveys of the investment literature pointedly illustrate this fact:

> The empirical findings ... indicate that the interest rate is not important whether statistical inference, interviews, or questionnaires have been the method of investigation.[27]

---

[26] Proponents of this position would not necessarily hold that this argument is totally devastating to the case for monetary policy. It is still possible, via an application of the Quantity Theory, that changes in the money supply will influence the level of output and, thus, investment through the accelerator.

[27] Meyer and Kuh, *op. cit.*, p. 8.

Our analysis has done little to support the view that variation of parameters at the control of the monetary authority is likely to mitigate cyclical fluctuations in investment or to increase the aggregate amount of investment.... We can say that neither theory nor data support the broad claims of monetary policy proponents.[28]

Both of these studies add qualifying statements to these remarks,[29] but, even so, there is no doubt as to their conclusions with respect to the influence exerted by monetary policy on investment.

The inability of econometricians to detect a relationship between interest rates and investment—in the face of reams of theoretical literature to the contrary[30]—has been puzzling even to the investigators themselves.[31] It is felt that notwithstanding the statistical problems involved, some evidence linking investment to interest rates should be forthcoming.

The impact of these past findings cannot be underestimated. There has been increasing pressure for fiscal maneuvers to augment and supplant efforts by the monetary authorities to control movements in economic activity. The growing reliance on fiscal action is particularly evident in those instances in recent years when the economy found itself

---

[28] R. Eisner and R. Stotz, *Determinants of Business Investment,* study paper for the Commision on Money and Credit, Chapter 5.

[29] Thus, Meyer and Kuh later add: "While the conclusions are not as absolutely one-sided as is often suggested, the existing body of empirical knowledge does not lend much comfort to the marginalist theories." Eisner and Stotz qualify their statement above with: "We are not in a position to say that these claims are all unambiguously refuted." There is evidence that interest rates are tied to investment in the housing (R. Muth, *op. cit.*), railroad, and electric utility industries (L. Klein, "Studies in Investment Behavior," in *Conference on Business Cycles,* National Bureau of Economic Research, 1951) and there is some weak evidence at the level of individual manufacturing firms (Grunfeld, *op. cit.*). Also, Griliches found that investment in at least one type of agricultural equipment was strongly related to interest rates (Z. Griliches, "The Demand for a Durable Input: Farm Tractors in the United States," pp. 181–207 in *The Demand for Durable Goods,* Harberger, *op. cit.*)

[30] The position of neoclassical theory in this respect is clearly outlined in Lutz and Lutz, *The Theory of Investment of the Firm, op. cit.*

[31] Thus, Klein and Goldberger (*op. cit.*) write: "Potentially we look with favor toward a significant role of interest rates in the investment equation but . . . we have not yet been able to make a reasonable judgment about its effect and cannot assign it a reliable nonzero value in this relation . . .. Perhaps the split at a later stage into residential construction, industrial construction, producers' equipment, and inventories will elucidate the significance of interest rates in 'real' economic behavior" (p. 12).

in recession. Certainly one major reason the role of business-cycle moderator has been gradually shifted from monetary to fiscal policy is the lack of evidence supporting the effectiveness of monetary policy.

Thus, the results reported in Chapter 4 take on an almost singular significance. The fact that we did find a definite, direct relationship between investment and interest rates sharply distinguishes our results from many previous studies. The interest elasticities of investment, calculated at the mean, which are implied by the interest rate coefficients of the long-run and short-run models are −.5 and −.3, respectively. These estimates were confirmed by further empirical efforts designed to obtain direct measures of the elasticities.[32]

---

[32] In order to obtain direct estimates of the elasticities, multiplicative approximations to the linear functional forms which underlie equations (11) and (25), Chapter 4, were estimated. These approximations are linear in the logarithms of the variables, whose coefficients can then be directly estimated by regression analysis. Since the elasticities we seek may be calculated as the ratio of the logs of investment and interest rates, the estimated regression coefficient for the log of the interest rate will serve as an estimate of the relevant elasticity over the entire period as opposed to one arbitrary point (i.e., the mean).

The results of these two tests are as follows:

$$\ln I_t = -2.78 + .92 \ln W_t + .49 \ln [\rho \ (.185) - r]_t,$$
$$(t = 14.7) \qquad (t = 18.2)$$
$$\bar{R}^2 = .925, \qquad d = .67;$$

$$\ln I_t = -1.79 + .59 \ln W_t + .32 \ln [\rho \ (.185) - r]_t + .37 \ln I_{t-1},$$
$$(t = 5.6) \qquad (t = 5.9) \qquad\qquad (t = 3.7)$$
$$\bar{R}^2 = .944, \qquad d = .85.$$

For several years during the thirties, yields were less than interest rates. Since the logs of negative numbers are undefined, a value of .01 was arbitrarily substituted for the variable whenever it became negative. Since investment tended to fall in those years when negative values occurred, by thus limiting the extent to which this variable was allowed to vary we have unavoidably introduced a slight negative bias into the estimate of the regression coefficients.

Two points are immediately evident from inspection of these two regression equations. *First*, the elasticities estimated from the logarithmic equations are virtually identical with the point estimates. Thus, on the basis of these results, we may consider the partial elasticity of investment with respect to the interest rate to approximate −.5 in the long run and −.3 in a year. *Second*, these two elasticities differ, as we should expect. Because of the time required to change plans, break habits, disseminate information, generate different projects, etc., economic functions grow more elastic as the time period over which they are defined lengthens. Thus, our results are consistent according to this additional criterion.

We have thus obtained important evidence that the actions of the monetary authorities can directly alter the level of investment expenditures. With an open market operation, the authorities have the ability to change the interest rate on government securities, which is eventually reflected in the rates on other financial instruments as well. We have found that changes in the rate on corporate bonds will affect the volume of investment according to the elasticities given above.[33]

However, as mentioned above, in the larger theoretical context the case for monetary policy in regulating investment activity does not depend exclusively on the direct interest elasticity of investment. For example, if, as a result of actions by the monetary authorities, the quantity of money demanded is not equal to the quantity of money supplied, interest rates will change as this market is brought into equilibrium. The yields on financial instruments will change correspondingly, altering the structure of yields on the various components of the asset portfolios held by economic units. Modifications will then occur in desired portfolios. Attempts to adjust actual stocks of assets to their newly desired levels will operate through the relative price mechanism to induce changes in economic activity, as discussed previously. It is not necessary that we be able to trace a direct linkage between a change in the yield of one particular asset (e.g., interest rates) to changes in investment. Even in the absence of a direct relationship, such changes may be linked through movements which are induced in one or more interjacent variables.

Our results are of interest in indicating that changes in the yields on bonds do, in fact, exert significant direct effects on the level of investment activity. Thus, aside from the indirect effects which can only be traced through a complete, simultaneously determined model of the economic system, changes in monetary policy designed to alter the

---

[33] The implications of these estimates of the interest elasticity of investment on employment and income are quite substantial. Consider, for example, the effect of action by the monetary authorities which would cause a change in interest rates of, say, .5 per cent. The Moody's Aa rate has averaged approximately 4.5 per cent over the past decade. Thus, the assumed change would represent, in percentage terms, a variation of 11 per cent on average. In the interest of conservatism, assume $-.3$. Then a drop in interest rates of .5 per cent implies an accompanying increase in investment expenditures of $-.3 \times -11$ per cent $= 3.3$ per cent, or \$1.16 billion, since the average level of private gross nonagricultural expenditures in recent years has been approximately \$35 billion. Through the multiplier, the effects on income and employment of an increase in investment of this magnitude will be magnified. Of course, to evaluate the complete effects of this change in interest rates, the added stimulus provided to investment in housing, inventories, etc. must also be considered.

money supply will initiate direct changes in investment expenditures to the extent that such policies cause changes to occur in the level of yields returned by financial assets.

The implications of various fiscal policies can also be traced with the portfolio-balance framework. Assume an increase in expenditures by the Treasury which is not accompanied by increased revenues through taxes. These expenditures will thus be financed by an exogenous increase in the supply of government bonds. Interest rates will thereby increase, and our results show that this will tend to have a depressing effect on private investment. Of course, to the extent that these expenditures enhance the earnings potential of private business, this tendency will be reversed. For example, an irrigation project which opens new markets will increase the expected yield on capital applied to the production of those goods sold in these markets, and thus tend to increase the desired stock of capital goods.

A change in the tax rate on business profits will directly affect the expected after-tax yield on assets, and the relationships between the yields on different assets. For instance, a reduction in the tax rate would tend to reduce the relative attractiveness of tax-free municipal securities, thus fostering the allocation of wealth into alternative assets. In the empirical tests of the present study, the profits variable was measured in pretax terms. However, it is income on an after-tax basis which actually accrues to the economic unit. Thus, it seems reasonable that in an expanded version of the model, in which consideration is given to alterations in the tax structure, the effects indicated above will be encountered.[34]

A final implication which can be drawn from the preceding discussion relates to the recent conception that monetary policy can be used to manage money and the gold flow while the real variables of the system (e.g., employment, investment, income) are controlled by fiscal policy.[35] This notion depends on the proposition that investment is virtually completely inelastic with respect to interest rates. Our results have shown that this premise is untrue. Our theoretical framework also reveals that it is impossible to separate neatly the effects of changes in monetary and fiscal policies into "financial" and "real" categories.

---

[34] Corresponding effects should accompany similar revisions in the laws governing tax credits, accelerated depreciation, etc.

[35] E.g., "Meanwhile, the tool of monetary policy is available to protect the dollar's international position while fiscal stimulus in reasonable degree does its work domestically." *The Morgan Guaranty Survey*, January 1963, p. 4, Morgan Guaranty Trust Company, New York.

Economic activity depends on the yields on all assets held in private portfolios. Thus, repercussions in both the financial and real sectors of the economy can be expected to accompany any policies which alter the structure of relative yields on privately held assets.

D. Concluding Remarks

This study was originally conceived as possessing a double purpose—one empirical, the other essentially theoretical. We were interested in devising a model of investment expenditures which would help to explain the wide fluctuations which have characterized past levels of the investment expenditures made by private business. In addition, it was desired to relate these specific results to a larger theoretical view of the economic system such that interrelationships between investment and activity in other areas of the economy could be better appreciated.

The investment equation which was derived from our model of the firm in Chapter 3 was found in the succeeding chapter to explain virtually all the variation in the investment data of private business. The parameters of the equation were consistent with the qualitative implications of the model, and interest rates were found to be an important determinant of investment expenditures. The predictive efficiency of the model is satisfactory, but extensions along the lines indicated in section A2 above will almost certainly improve its ability in this area. Thus, on the basis of the evidence we have found, our approach to the empirical questions in which we were interested has been reasonably successful.

Our model of the firm can be viewed as part of the larger conceptual framework provided by the general theory of portfolio balancing. In this theory, changes in the asset structure of the portfolio held by a given economic unit depend on the yields being returned by portfolio components. The view provided by this theory is substantially more comprehensive than those of alternative models of the investment decision. In addition, this theory was found to possess profound implications for the management of monetary and fiscal policy. The fundamental characteristic which distinguishes portfolio-balance theory from other models of economic processes is the central role that is given to stocks of various assets and wealth rather than to the flows to which movements in these stocks give rise. An important conclusion which can be drawn from this study of investment behavior is that stock-flow relationships must receive the emphasis now usually given to flows alone if we are to gain a satisfactory understanding of the processes which underlie changes in economic activity.

APPENDIX

The Data

This appendix describes the sources of the data and methods of compilation employed in deriving estimates of the time series of the variables used in this study. For the benefit of future researchers, the actual estimates of all these series are given in the pages following the explanations. Where relevant, the component series of final variables used in the text are also included when it is thought they might be useful. Discussion of the derivation procedures for each variable precedes the presentation of the estimates.

Three frequently cited sources are abbreviated. These sources are:

(1) *Historical Statistics of the United States, Colonial Times to 1957*, Department of Commerce, Washington, D.C., 1960. Abbreviation: *Hist. Stat.*

(2) Goldsmith, R. M., *A Study of Saving in the United States*, Princeton University Press, Princeton, N.J., 1953 (Three Volumes). Abbreviation: Goldsmith, *Saving*.

(3) Terborgh, G., *60 Years of Business Capital Formation*, Machinery and Allied Products Institute, Council for Technological Advancement, Washington, D.C., 1960. Abbreviation: MAPI, *60 Years*.

Col. (1), V^S: Market value, at beginning of year, of all outstanding shares of U.S. Corporations (billions of dollars)

1915–1923: Goldsmith, in Supplementary Appendix F-4 to *Financial Intermediaries in the American Economy Since 1900*, has given estimates of the value of outstanding corporate securities for eight benchmark dates from 1900–1949. Estimates for the years between these benchmarks were obtained by interpolating according to the movements of Standard and Poor's index of Common Stock Prices (series X-351 in *Hist. Stat.*). Let S_0, S_n, and I_n be Goldsmith's estimate at the base year (0), Goldsmith's estimate at the next base year (n), and the Standard and Poor's index at the end base year (n), respectively. Then the esti-

117

mates for the intervening years ($\hat{S}_t$) were obtained from the formula

$$\hat{S}_t = S_{t-1} + \frac{S_n - S_{t-1}}{n - (t - 1)} \left(\frac{I_t}{I_n} \right),$$

for $t = 1, 2, \ldots, n - 1$. Thus, the movements in market price, as reflected in the price index, determine what proportion of the difference between the end base year (S_n) and the previous year (S_{t-1}) will be made up in the current year.

1924–1945: The Goldsmith benchmarks were interpolated by movements in the value of all corporate shares listed on the New York Stock Exchange (*Fact Book, 1959*). Denote the ratio at the base year of the Goldsmith estimate, S, to the New York Stock Exchange figure, V, by r_0 and by r_n for the next base year. Then the annual estimates were obtained by

$$\hat{S}_t = \frac{n - t}{n} \left[r_0 + \frac{t}{n} r_n \right] V_t,$$

for $t = 1, 2, \ldots, n - 1$.

1946–1961: Market value of corporate stock from *Flow of Funds/Saving Accounts, 1946–1960, Supplement 5*, Federal Reserve System, December 1961. Table 7, line IV-G.

Col. (2), V^B: Market value, at beginning of year, of all bonds of U.S. Corporations (billions of dollars)

Corporate bonds outstanding valued at par were obtained from 1915 to 1950 (end-of-year figures) from W. B. Hickman, *The Volume of Corporate Bond Financing Since 1900*, Appendix A, Table A-1. From 1951 to 1961, the figures were obtained from *Flow of Funds/Savings Accounts, Supplement 5*, Table 25L, line B. These series are directly comparable. (The five years of overlapping data from the two series agree precisely, indicating that the same sources and methods of compilation were used in both.) The market value of corporate bonds is then estimated by multiplying the par values by Standard and Poor's index (base = 100) of corporate bond prices (1915–1958, *Hist. Stat.*, series X350; 1959–1961, Federal Reserve Bulletin, August 1961).

The Standard and Poor's index of bond prices is a conversion of yield indices assuming a 4 per cent coupon with 20 years to maturity. Thus, although the yields themselves are not based on bonds of constant 20-year maturity, the conversion to prices is so characterized. Since the data of aggregate par value of bonds contain bonds of various maturities, some inconsistencies are introduced by this conversion process.

However, while these inconsistencies imply that the price index is not a perfect reflection of the information on yields, at least the conversion process provides a monotonic transformation of the yield data. Thus, the error incurred by this procedure probably is not of inordinate magnitude. At any rate, certainly this procedure provides better estimates of the market value of bonds than would utilization of the unadjusted par values alone.

Col. (3), V: Market value, at beginning of year, of all outstanding securities of U.S. corporations (billions of dollars)

Col. (1) + Col. (2)

Col. (4), r: Average interest rate on corporate bonds (per cent).

1915–1918: Unadjusted index number of yields of American railroad bonds (*Hist. Stat.*, series X332) raised by an adjustment factor of 1.34. This factor is the average quotient obtained by dividing Moody's estimate of the interest rate, used for 1919–1961, by the railroad bond index for the years in which the two series overlap (1919–1936).

1919–1961: Moody's composite average of yields on corporate bonds pp. a19-a20, *Industrial Manual*, 1961.

Col. (5), rV^B: Interest expense of U.S. corporations (billions of dollars)

1915–1960: Col. (4) × Col. (2), end of year.

Col. (6), π: Corporate net pretax earnings (billions of dollars)

1915: Goldsmith, *Saving*, Table C-26, Vol. I.

1916–1922: Goldsmith, *Saving*, Table C-28, Vol. I.

1923–1960: *Statistics of Income*, Bureau of Internal Revenue, various editions.

Col. (7), X: Gross return on corporate assets (billions of dollars)

1915–1960: Col. (5) + Col. (6).

Col. (8), K^G: Stock of plant and equipment, beginning of year, held by nonagricultural business using linear retirement curves (billions of dollars)

1915–1944: The stock of business capital in plant and equipment held by unincorporated business and nonfinancial corporations is estimated by Goldsmith, *Saving*, for benchmark years in Tables W-29 and W-31 (Vol. III), respectively. Let these estimates in the base year, 0, and at the next benchmark, n years later, be denoted as K_0 and K_n.

Then the estimates $(\hat{K}_t)$ for intervening years were obtained from the formula

$$\hat{K}_t = \left[\frac{n - t}{n} \frac{K_0}{W_0} + \frac{t}{n} \frac{K_n}{W_n} \right] W_t \quad (t = 1, 2, \ldots, n - 1),$$

where W_t is Goldsmith's (yearly) estimate of national wealth approximately defined as the sum of the tangible assets of the component sectors of the economy. This series is given in Table W-1, Vol. III.

1945–1959: Unpublished data from the forthcoming study by Goldsmith and Lipsey. Permission was received from Professor Goldsmith to use these data in the study.

Col. (9), I: Gross expenditures by private nonagricultural business on plant and equipment (billions of dollars)

1915–1944: Col. (10) + Col. (12)

1945–1961: Department of Commerce-Securities and Exchange Commission, reported in *Survey of Current Business*, June 1956, March 1958, March 1960, and March 1962. These figures exclude expenditures by agricultural business and those charged to current account.

Col. (10), C: Gross expenditures by private nonagricultural business on plant (billions of dollars)

1915–1961: The sum of the expenditures on new plant by six business groups, covering approximately all nonfinancial business, as tabulated in *Construction Volume and Costs 1915–1956* and subsequent issues of the *Construction Review*. The pre-1920 figures were extrapolated backward by MAPI for *60 Years*. Construction expenditures by the agricultural sector are included in these extrapolations. Thus, agricultural expenditures on business construction, as given by Goldsmith, *Saving*, Table A-7, Vol. I, were subtracted from the MAPI estimates.

Col. (11), C^M: Gross investment in plant by private business, using nonlinear retirement curve (billions of dollars)

1915–1961: An alternative estimate of the capital stock is provided by assuming nonlinear retirements of plant and equipment, as recommended by MAPI. Estimates of the stock of plant and equipment (C^M and C^E) obtained under one such assumption are found through the application of survival percentages to date on the past installations in constant 1954 dollars. The estimated percentages of original installations surviving after given intervals is based on a retirement distribution which is symmetric around average service life, worked out for a considerable number of recorded retirement age observations by R. Winfrey, *Statistical Analysis of Industrial Property Retirements,* Iowa Engineering Experiment Station, Bulletin 125. The particular curve used is Winfrey's "S_3" curve, which is assumed by MAPI to adequately represent the distribution for all types of investment on average. The "S_3" retirement distribution is a frequency function of the form

$$(A.1) \qquad y_x = y_0 \left[1 - \left(\frac{x}{10} \right)^2 \right]^b,$$

where

x = age measured from average life $(\bar{x})$ in units equal to 10 per cent of average life,

y_x = fraction depleted at period x,

y_0 = .156105,

b = 6.90159.

The average service life (x) for construction is given by MAPI as 50 years in the Statistical Supplement to *60 Years.* [This figure was obtained by a weighted combination of the individual service lives listed in the U.S. Internal Revenue Service "Bulletin F" (1942) for a large number of types of plant.]

To transform (A.1) so that the units are years, not decile units, we define

$$(A.2) \qquad x = \frac{t - \bar{x}}{(\bar{x}/10)} \qquad (t = 0, 1, \ldots, 2\bar{x}).$$

The range of t follows from the fact that (A.1) is a Beta-function, as shown below. Substituting (A.2) into (A.1), we find

$$(A.3) \qquad y_t = \frac{10y_0}{\bar{x}} \left[1 - \left(\frac{t - \bar{x}}{\bar{x}} \right)^2 \right]^b,$$

from which the fraction surviving at the end of the tth year following installation, θ_t, is

$$(A.4) \qquad \theta_t = 1 - \int_0^t y_t \, dt$$

$$= 1 - \left\{ \frac{10y_0}{\bar{x}} \int_0^t \left[1 - \left(\frac{t - \bar{x}}{\bar{x}} \right)^2 \right]^b dt \right\}.$$

Because of the symmetry of this function, we need only calculate θ

for $0 \leq t \leq \bar{x}$, since $\theta_{t-\bar{x}} = 1 - \theta_t$. Thus, the argument, t, in (A.4) has the range $0 \leq t \leq x$.

That the integral of (A.4) is a Beta-function can be shown by letting

(A.5) $$u = 1 - \left(\frac{t - \bar{x}}{\bar{x}}\right)^2, \qquad 0 \leq u \leq 1,$$

from which

$$du = -2\left(\frac{t - \bar{x}}{\bar{x}}\right) dt$$

$$= -2(1 - u)^{.5} dt,$$

or

(A.6) $$dt = \frac{-(1 - u)^{-.5}}{2} du.$$

Substitution of (A.5) and (A.6) into the integral of (A.4) yields

(A.5) $$\int_0^t \left[1 - \left(\frac{t - \bar{x}}{\bar{x}}\right)^2\right]^b dt = \int_0^u u^b(1 - u)^{-.5} du,$$

which can be calculated from tables of the incomplete Beta-function, $B_u(b + 1, \frac{1}{2})$.

In fact, the integral of (A.4) was evaluated by Simpson's Rule, which gives an approximation to any desired accuracy of a definite integral for most reasonably well-behaved curves. In this case, the integral was broken into 200 subintervals and the estimated θ_t are accurate to five decimal places.

Given the θ_t, annual construction expenditures before 1915 are needed for 100 years ($= 2\bar{x}$), although $\theta_t < .005$ for $t \geq 80$. Thus, pre-1835 estimates are, for practical purposes, largely irrelevant. The estimates were obtained as follows:

1900–1914: MAPI (based on W. H. Shaw, *Value of Commodity Output Since 1949*), supplement to *60 Years*, less construction expenditures by the agricultural sector obtained from Goldsmith, *Saving*, Table A-7, Vol. I.

1869–1899: S. Kuznets, in technical tables underlying *Capital in the American Economy: Its Formation and Financing*, provides estimates of nonresidential, private investment for 1869–1955 (p. 17; these tables were made available by the National Bureau of Economic Research). This series was spliced with that of the present study, the latter controlling as to level.

Pre-1869: Attempts to relate both the present, post-1869, series and the Kuznets series to (a) trend, (b) the price index of building material relative to that of all products, (c) the price index of building materials alone, and (d) deviations from "normal," as estimated by the Cleveland Trust Company (*American Business Activity Since 1890,* 1959 edition), all proved fruitless. Although the relationships were sometimes significant, extrapolations backward gave meaningless results (i.e., negative expenditures) after several periods.

Thus, a less sophisticated but very straightforward method of estimation was used to obtain the pre-1869 estimates. It was found that the average growth per year in the (constant-dollar) expenditures was approximately 3 per cent. The five-year average, centered at 1871 of our estimates, was taken as "normal" for 1871 and was used as a base from which estimates of prior expenditures were obtained by decreasing this figure by 3 per cent per year.

A partial check on the accuracy of the post-1859 data is provided by comparing the estimate of the capital stock in 1899 that is obtained using linear depreciation and a 50-year average service life with the estimate given by Goldsmith (*Saving*), who invokes similar assumptions. The Goldsmith figure in 1929 dollars is $24.2 billion and that implied by the estimates described above is $25.1 billion, a deviation of less than 4 per cent. This result suggests that the estimated annual figures are at least broadly consistent with those used by Goldsmith.

The estimates were converted to 1954 dollars, using the deflator of Col. (15). A lengthy correction for fire losses was introduced, but the effect on the final estimates was too insignificant to merit comment.

Col. (12), E: Gross expenditures on equipment by private nonagricultural business (billions of dollars)

1915–1961: Through 1928 the data are those compiled for private business by MAPI (supplement to *60 Years*) less expenditures on durable equipment by the agricultural sector, obtained from *Hist. Stat. 1789–1945,* Series E-108. Starting in 1929 the figures are those of the Department of Commerce series of private purchases of producers' durable equipment less capital outlays charged to current expense and expenditures by agriculture, obtained from *Hist. Stat. 1789–1945* and *Statistical Abstract of the United States,* various editions.

Note that I [Col. (9)] is equal to C [Col. (10)] plus E [Col. (12)] previous to 1945 (except for rounding), but not thereafter. The Commerce-SEC series used for I after and including 1945 is not broken down into plant and equipment. The separate series on C and E were needed, however, for the calculations of P^K [Col. (16)], and may be useful to later researchers. The difference between I and $C + E$ for the post-1944 period are generally quite small. The median absolute discrepancy between the two series for the sixteen years 1945–1960 is 4.3 per cent. The maximum discrepancy occurs in 1945 (16.6 per cent), but since this year was not included in the study because of the disturbing effects created by the war, this rather large difference does not influence our results.

Col. (13), E^M: Gross investment in equipment by private nonagricultural business using nonlinear retirement curve (billions of dollars)

1915–1961: These estimates were obtained using the same method as in the estimation of C^M, Col. (11). Here the average life, $\bar{x}$, of durable equipment is taken as 17 years, estimated by MAPI from a weighted average of many types of durable equipment whose average lives are given in the Bureau of Internal Revenue "Bulletin F" (1942). Expenditures for the 34 years (i.e., $2\bar{x}$) between 1881 and 1915 were estimated as follows:

1900–1914: MAPI, supplement to *60 Years*, less expenditures by agriculture obtained 1900–1909 from Goldsmith, *Saving*, Table A-16, Vol. 1, and for 1910–1914 from *Hist. Stat., 1789–1945*, Series E-108.

1881–1899: These estimates were provided by Kuznets (*Capital in the American Economy*, technical tables, p. 23). They were then spliced with the 1900–1914 estimates, the latter controlling as to level.

Col. (14), K^M: Gross investment by private, nonagricultural business using nonlinear retirement curves (billions of dollars)

1915–1961: Col. (11) + Col. (13).

Col. (15), P: Price deflator for privately produced gross national product, 1954 = 100

1915–1959: MAPI, implicit index in supplement to *60 Years of Business Capital Formation*, converted to 1954 = 100.

1960–1961: This deflator was obtained by taking the ratio of privately produced gross national product in constant and current dollars (recent issues of *Survey of Current Business*).

Col. (16), P^K: Price deflator for physical investment goods of private business, 1954 = 100

This is a weighted average of price of equipment and price of construction, where the weights are the proportion of the total investment undertaken in equipment [Col. (12)] and plant [Col. (10)], respectively. The price of equipment was obtained from a splice of the series given by Goldsmith, *Saving*, Table P-5, Vol. I, and that of the Department of Commerce (*Economic Report of the President*, 1962, Table B-6). The price of business construction was similarly obtained from a splice of Goldsmith (*Saving*, p. 609, Vol. I) and Commerce series (*Economic Report*, Table B-6).

Col. (17), P^L: Index of average hourly earnings, manufacturing industries, 1954 = 100

The series on average hourly earnings in manufacturing industries was converted to an index with 1954 = 100. The earning figures were obtained from:

1915–1938: Hist. Stat., series D-626.

1939–1961: Economic Report of the President, 1961, Table B-28.

Col. (18), N^U: Percentage of the labor force which is unemployed (unemployment rate)

1915–1956: Hist. Stat., series D-47.

1957–1961: A change in the definitions of employment and unemployment in 1957 resulted in between 200,000 and 300,000 workers formerly classified as employed being counted as unemployed. In the interests of preserving consistency in the series used, an adjustment for this reclassification was made to the post-1956 unemployment figures by subtracting 250,000 from the reported unemployment total. Total work force and unemployment for post-1956 were obtained from *Economic Report of the President*, 1961, Table B-20.

Col. (19), D^F: Diffusion index of leading indicators (per cent), average of last six months of previous year

1915–1919: Business Cycle Indicators, National Bureau of Economics Research, G. H. Moore, ed., Vol. II, series D 50.3 (75 leading series).

1920–1959: Business Cycle Indicators, Vol. II, series D 50.0 (8 leading series).

1960–1961: These figures were compiled from basic data on the eight component series used in D 50.0 for 1920–1959. These basic data are contained in *Business Cycle Developments*, Department of Commerce, April 1962.

The Data

Col:	(1)	(2)	(3)	(4)	(5)	(6)	(7)	(8)
	V^S	V^B	V	r	$_rV^B$	π	X	K^G
1915	43.0	16.6	59.6	6.19	1.03	5.31	6.34	39.55
1916	46.0	16.6	62.6	6.62	1.03	8.10	9.13	43.36
1917	49.5	17.1	66.6	6.42	1.08	10.10	11.18	51.49
1918	52.5	16.8	69.3	7.01	1.12	7.67	8.79	62.57
1919	55.2	16.0	71.2	6.27	1.01	8.42	9.43	72.01
1920	58.4	16.1	74.5	7.08	1.10	5.87	6.97	85.78
1921	61.9	15.6	77.5	7.04	1.18	.46	1.64	86.48
1922	64.2	16.7	80.9	5.95	1.14	4.77	5.91	76.23
1923	67.5	19.2	86.7	6.04	1.20	6.31	7.51	77.94
1924	70.0	20.0	90.0	5.80	1.25	5.36	6.61	83.14
1925	75.6	21.6	97.2	5.47	1.25	7.62	8.87	85.48
1926	95.9	22.8	118.7	5.21	1.26	7.50	8.76	89.17
1927	106.4	24.6	131.0	4.97	1.34	6.51	7.85	92.46
1928	137.2	26.9	164.1	4.94	1.35	8.23	9.58	95.77
1929	185.6	27.4	213.0	5.21	1.39	8.74	10.13	99.47
1930	177.9	26.7	204.6	5.09	1.45	1.55	3.00	101.31
1931	127.9	28.5	156.4	5.81	1.71	−3.29	−1.58	95.39
1932	66.5	29.4	95.9	6.87	1.81	−5.64	−3.83	84.81
1933	53.8	26.3	77.1	5.89	1.62	−2.55	−.93	77.33
1934	73.8	27.5	101.3	4.96	1.44	.10	1.54	79.97
1935	74.6	29.0	103.6	4.46	1.35	1.69	3.04	81.26
1936	101.8	30.3	132.1	3.87	1.21	7.33	8.54	80.43
1937	128.2	31.3	159.5	3.94	1.20	7.35	8.55	83.84
1938	81.7	30.5	112.2	4.19	1.32	3.68	5.00	85.95
1939	98.3	31.4	129.7	3.77	1.20	6.74	7.94	84.45
1940	95.0	31.7	126.7	3.55	1.13	8.92	10.05	85.13
1941	83.0	31.9	116.9	3.34	1.05	16.73	17.78	88.65
1942	72.7	31.5	104.2	3.34	1.04	23.05	23.09	95.98
1943	78.4	31.0	109.4	3.16	.95	27.83	28.78	99.41
1944	95.7	30.0	125.7	3.05	.89	26.30	27.19	99.72
1945	111.6	29.3	140.9	2.87	.82	21.14	21.96	99.35
1946	119.	28.6	148.	2.74	.82	25.19	26.01	101.90
1947	111.	30.1	141.	2.86	.95	31.42	32.37	128.44
1948	109.	33.2	142.	3.08	1.14	34.43	35.57	155.78
1949	108.	37.1	145.	2.96	1.23	28.20	29.43	176.71
1950	120.	41.4	161.	2.86	1.24	42.61	43.85	183.52
1951	146.	43.5	190.	3.08	1.41	43.55	44.96	208.02
1952	170.	45.8	216.	3.19	1.60	38.46	40.06	229.05
1953	186.	50.3	236.	3.43	1.80	39.49	41.29	243.46
1954	179.	52.4	231.	3.16	1.78	36.33	38.11	260.28
1955	258.	56.2	314.	3.25	1.96	47.48	49.44	274.27
1956	317.	60.4	377.	3.57	2.20	46.89	49.19	292.69
1957	338.	61.5	400.	4.21	2.67	44.48	47.15	325.53
1958	299.	63.4	362.	4.16	2.93	38.52	41.45	362.94
1959	418.	70.4	478.	4.65	3.16	46.77	49.93	378.86
1960	454.	68.0	522.	4.73	3.34	45.04	48.38	
1961	442.	70.6	513.	4.66				

Col:	(9)	(10)	(11)	(12)	(13)	(14)	(15)
	I	C	C^M	E	E^M	K^M	P
1915	2.24	1.13	39.49	1.11	16.24	55.73	37.2
1916	3.58	1.46	41.81	2.12	17.29	59.09	41.8
1917	4.58	1.65	48.24	2.94	20.81	69.05	52.6
1918	5.22	1.72	61.67	3.50	27.98	89.65	62.1
1919	5.01	1.92	73.69	3.10	35.11	108.80	67.2
1920	6.13	2.61	80.82	3.52	39.52	120.34	78.4
1921	4.08	1.85	93.10	2.23	46.39	139.49	63.1
1922	4.35	1.99	78.08	2.34	39.01	117.09	57.6
1923	6.18	2.61	72.43	3.57	36.42	108.85	59.0
1924	5.95	2.74	75.87	3.21	39.12	114.99	58.8
1925	6.32	2.92	77.44	3.40	40.57	118.01	59.6
1926	7.17	3.42	80.42	3.75	42.73	123.15	58.8
1927	6.92	3.47	81.81	3.45	44.10	125.91	57.8
1928	7.19	3.46	82.58	3.73	44.80	127.39	58.5
1929	8.39	3.83	86.26	4.56	47.29	133.56	58.4
1930	6.63	3.11	88.97	3.53	49.82	138.78	56.3
1931	3.97	1.73	87.84	2.24	49.55	137.40	50.4
1932	2.00	.82	79.41	1.19	44.73	124.17	45.3
1933	1.81	.63	71.33	1.18	39.63	110.96	44.6
1934	2.41	.74	70.00	1.68	38.42	108.42	47.4
1935	3.06	.77	74.21	2.28	40.53	114.74	48.0
1936	4.16	1.11	74.92	3.05	41.23	116.16	48.1
1937	5.32	1.60	75.20	3.71	42.20	117.39	50.0
1938	3.68	1.18	78.69	2.51	45.23	123.93	49.1
1939	4.27	1.28	77.40	2.99	44.56	121.95	48.5
1940	5.94	1.62	76.63	4.32	44.56	121.19	49.3
1941	6.39	2.15	78.38	5.24	47.08	125.47	53.9
1942	4.21	1.33	86.60	2.89	53.89	140.48	61.3
1943	3.51	.78	98.34	2.73	60.89	159.23	67.7
1944	4.47	1.02	107.71	3.45	66.30	174.01	81.0
1945	8.69	1.68	127.95	5.57	78.41	206.36	69.4
1946	14.85	5.11	109.45	9.64	68.93	178.37	75.2
1947	20.61	5.79	121.75	13.44	80.26	202.01	83.9
1948	22.06	5.88	139.27	14.08	98.43	237.70	89.5
1949	19.28	5.54	152.06	12.25	114.37	266.43	88.8
1950	20.60	5.93	153.92	13.98	121.02	274.94	89.9
1951	25.64	7.57	159.14	15.24	131.70	290.84	97.0
1952	26.49	7.83	176.49	15.46	152.20	328.69	98.7
1953	28.32	8.84	184.52	16.80	164.97	349.49	99.2
1954	26.83	8.97	191.36	17.55	177.10	368.46	100.0
1955	28.70	10.50	198.81	17.54	190.28	389.09	100.8
1956	35.08	11.92	207.79	21.52	203.25	411.04	103.6
1957	36.96	12.94	222.16	22.98	223.76	445.92	107.6
1958	30.53	11.49	240.34	17.81	248.21	488.54	109.3
1959	32.54	11.49	252.01	20.18	261.97	513.98	110.8
1960	35.68	12.80	263.34	23.55	277.16	540.50	113.0
1961	34.37		277.66		296.79	574.46	113.6

	Col.: (16)	(17)	(18)	(19)
	P^K	P^L	N^u	D^J
1915	25.9	15.2	9.7	33.8
1916	31.0	18.5	4.8	96.6
1917	39.2	21.3	4.8	66.6
1918	50.5	24.2	1.4	32.3
1919	54.4	27.0	2.3	22.4
1920	60.0	31.5	4.0	77.8
1921	49.0	29.2	11.9	4.2
1922	44.4	27.5	7.6	80.4
1923	47.7	29.2	3.2	73.8
1924	46.9	30.9	5.5	56.3
1925	47.1	30.9	4.0	85.4
1926	47.0	30.9	1.9	79.2
1927	46.4	30.9	4.1	45.8
1928	46.7	31.5	4.4	74.0
1929	47.5	32.0	3.2	53.1
1930	45.4	30.9	8.7	14.6
1931	42.8	29.2	15.9	14.6
1932	39.9	25.3	23.6	10.4
1933	39.2	24.7	24.9	41.7
1934	42.1	29.8	21.7	50.0
1935	43.0	30.9	20.1	72.9
1936	42.7	31.5	16.9	85.4
1937	46.0	34.8	14.3	89.6
1938	46.7	35.4	19.0	2.1
1939	46.1	35.4	17.2	84.4
1940	47.5	37.1	14.6	72.9
1941	50.6	41.0	9.9	75.0
1942	55.1	47.8	4.7	52.1
1943	57.4	53.9	1.9	56.3
1944	58.6	56.7	1.2	55.2
1945	59.3	57.3	1.9	61.5
1946	65.3	60.7	3.9	79.2
1947	76.2	68.5	3.6	34.4
1948	83.1	74.7	3.4	62.1
1949	85.6	77.5	5.5	2.1
1950	87.8	80.9	5.0	89.6
1951	95.6	87.6	3.0	61.5
1952	97.2	92.7	2.7	40.6
1953	99.0	97.8	2.5	58.3
1954	100.0	100.0	5.0	37.5
1955	102.8	104.5	4.0	83.3
1956	109.6	109.6	3.8	51.1
1957	115.7	115.2	3.9	42.7
1958	118.4	118.5	7.2	13.5
1959	121.5	123.0	5.8	82.3
1960	121.5	127.0	6.1	41.3
1961	121.5	130.3	7.2	20.8

Bibliography

1. Ackley, G., *Macroeconomic Theory*, New York: The Macmillan Company, 1961.

2. Allen, R. G. D., *Mathematical Economics*, London: The Macmillan Company, 1957.

3. Ando, A. K., *A Contribution to the Theory of Economic Fluctuations and Growth*, unpublished Ph.D. thesis, Carnegie Institute of Technology, April 1959.

4. Andrews, P. W. S., *Manufacturing Business*, London: The Macmillan Company, 1949.

5. ———, "A Further Inquiry into the Effects of Rates of Interests," *Oxford Economic Papers*, 1940, pp. 33–73.

6. ———, and E. Brunner, *Capital Development in Steel: A Study of the United States Steel Companies, Ltd.*, London: Oxford University Press, 1951.

7. Arrow, K. J., H. B. Chenery, B. M. Minhas, and R. M. Solow, "Capital-Labor Substitution and Economic Efficiency," *Review of Economics and Statistics*, 1961, pp. 225–251.

8. Bain, J. S., *Barriers to New Competition, Their Character and Consequences in Manufacturing Industries*, Cambridge, Mass.: Harvard University Press, 1956.

9. Bartlett, M. S., "The Fitting of Straight Lines If Both Variables are Subject to Error," *Biometrics*, 1949, pp. 207–242.

10. Baumol, W. J., "Income Effect, Substitution Effect, Ricardo Effect," Part II from "The Analogy Between Producer and Consumer Equilibrium Analysis," *Economica*, 1950, pp. 63–80.

11. Berle, A. A. Jr., and G. C. Means, *The Modern Corporation and Private Property*, New York: The Macmillan Company, 1934.

12. Bierman, H., and S. Schmidt, *The Capital Budgeting Decision*, New York: The Macmillan Company, 1960.

13. Brunner, K., "The Report of the Commission on Money and Credit," *Journal of Political Economy*, 1961, pp. 605–620.

14. Cagan, P., "The Monetary Dynamics of Hyperinflation," *Studies in the Quantity Theory of Money*, M. Friedman, ed., Chicago: University of Chicago Press, 1956, pp. 25–117.

15. Chenery, H. B., "Overcapacity and the Acceleration Principle," *Econometrica*, 1952, pp. 1–28.

16. Clark, J. M., "Business Acceleration and the Law of Demand: A Technical Factor in Economic Cycles," *Journal of Political Economy*, 1917.

17. Collins, N. R., and L. E. Preston, "The Size Structure of the Largest Industrial Firms, 1909–1958," *American Economic Review*, 1961, pp. 986–1003.

18. Denison, E. F., "Theoretical Aspects of Quality Change, Capital Consumption, and Net Capital Formation," *Problems of Capital Formation*, Vol. 19 of Studies in Income and Wealth, National Bureau of Economic Research, 1957, pp. 215–261.

19. ———, "Problems in the Theory of Capital," in Studies in Income and Wealth, Vol. 19, *Review of Economic Studies*, 1955–56.

20. Duesenberry, J. S., O. Eckstein, and G. Fromm, "A Simulation of the United States Economy in Recession," *Econometrica*, 1960, pp. 749–809.

21. Durbin, J., and G. S. Watson, "Testing for Serial Correlation in Least-Squares Regression," *Biometrika*, 1950 (Part I) and 1951 (Part II).

22. Ebersole, J. F., "The Influence of Interest Rates Upon Entrepreneurial Decisions in Business—A Case Study," *Harvard Business Review*, Autumn 1938, pp. 35–40.

23. Edwards, H. R., "Price Formation in Manufacturing Industry and Excess Capacity," *Oxford Economic Papers*, 1955, pp. 94–118.

24. Eisner, R., "Capital Expenditures, Profits and the Acceleration Principle," Preliminary version given at the Conference on Research in Income and Wealth, Febraury 2, 3, 1962, National Bureau of Economic Research.

25. ———, "A Distributed Lag Investment Function," *Econometrica*, 1960, pp. 1–30.

26. ———, "Interview and Other Survey Techniques and the Study of Investment," *Problems of Capital Formation*, National Bureau of Economic Research, 1957, pp. 513–584.

27. ———, "Expectations, Plans, and Capital Expenditures: A Synthesis of Ex Post and Ex Ante Data," *Expectations, Uncertainty and Business Behavior*, Social Science Research Council, M. J. Bowman, ed., pp. 49–58.

28. ———, and R. H. Strotz, *Determinants of Business Investment*, Commission on Money and Credit, 1962.

29. Ezekial, M., and K. A. Fox, *Methods of Correlation and Regression Analysis*, New York: John Wiley & Sons, Inc., 3rd ed., 1959.

30. Farrar, D. E., *The Investment Decision Under Uncertainty*, Englewood Cliffs, N. J.: Prentice-Hall, Inc., 1962.

31. Ferber, R., "Measuring the Accuracy and Structure of Businessmen's Expectations," *Journal of the American Statistical Association*, 1953, pp. 385–413.

32. Fisher, I., *Theory of Interest*, London: The Macmillan Company, 1930; reprinted, New York: Kelley and Millman, 1954.

33. Fisher, R. A., *Statistical Methods for Research Workers*, New York: Hafner Publishing Company, Inc., 13th ed., 1958.

34. Friedman, M., *A Theory of the Consumption Function*, National Bureau of Economic Research, New York, 1957.

35. ———, "The Quantity Theory of Money—A Restatement," chap. 1 in *Studies in the Quantity Theory of Money*, M. Friedman, ed., Chicago: University of Chicago Press, 1956.

36. Friend, I., and J. Bronfenbrenner, "Business Investment Programs and Their Realizations", *Survey of Current Business*, December 1950, pp. 11–22.

37. Goldsmith, R. W., *A Study of Savings in the United States*, Princeton, N. J.: Princeton University Press (3 vols.), 1953.

38. Gordon, M. J., *The Investment, Financing and Valuation of the Corporation*, Homewood, Ill.: Richard D. Irwin, Inc., 1962.

39. Gordon, R. A., "Differential Changes in the Prices of Consumers' and Capital Goods," *American Economic Review*, 1961, pp. 937–957.

40. ———, *Business Fluctuations*, New York: Harper & Row, Publishers, 1952.

41. Grunfeld, Y., "The Determinants of Capital Investment," *The Demand for Durable Goods*, A. C. Harberger, ed., Chicago: University of Chicago Press, 1960, pp. 211–266.

42. Gurley, J., and E. S. Shaw, *Money in a Theory of Finance*, Washington, D.C.: The Brookings Institution, 1960.

43. Haavelmo, T., "Remarks on Frisch's Confluence Analysis and Its Use in Econometrics," Chap. 5 in T. J. Koopmans, ed., *Statistical Inference in Dynamic Models*, New York: John Wiley & Sons, Inc., 1950.

44. ———, "The Effect of the Rate of Interest on Investment: A Note," *Review on Economic Statistics*, 1947, pp. 49–52.

45. Hald, A., *Statistical Theory with Engineering Applications*, New York: John Wiley & Sons, Inc., 1952.

46. Hauge, G., "Economic Growth: An American View," *Economic Growth—Balance of Payments*, The American Bankers Association, 1962, pp. 21–34.

47. Heller, W. W., "The Anatomy of Investment Decisions," *Harvard Business Review*, 1951, pp. 95–103.

48. ———, Hearings before the Joint Economic Committee on *Employment, Growth and Price Levels*, p. 2997.

49. Hicks, J. R., *A Contribution to the Theory of the Trade Cycle*, Oxford: Clarendon Press, 1950.

50. ———, *Value and Capital*, London: Oxford University Press, 2nd ed., 1946.

51. Johnston, J., *Econometric Methods*, New York: McGraw-Hill, Inc., 1963.

52. Kalecki, M., "The Principle of Increasing Risk," *Economica*, 1937, pp. 440–447.

53. ———, "A Theory of the Business Cycle," *Review of Economic Studies*, 1936, pp. 77–97.

54. Keezer, D. M., R. P. Ulin, D. Greenwald, and H. Matulis, "Observations on the Predictive Quality of McGraw-Hill Surveys of Business' Plans for New Plants and Equipment," *The Quality and Economic Significance of Anticipations Data,* New York: National Bureau of Economic Research, 1960, pp. 369–385.

55. Keynes, J. M., *The General Theory of Employment, Interest and Money,* London: Harcourt, Brace & World, Inc., 1936.

56. Kisselgoff, A., and F. Modigliani, "Private Investment in the Electric Power Industry and the Acceleration Principle," *Review of Economics and Statistics,* 1957, pp. 363–379.

57. Klein, L. R., "Studies in Investment Behavior," *Conference on Business Cycles,* National Bureau of Economic Research, 1951.

58. ———, *Economic Fluctuations in the United States, 1921–1941,* New York: John Wiley & Sons, Inc., 1950.

59. ———, and A. S. Goldberger, *An Econometric Model of the United States, 1929–1952,* Amsterdam: North-Holland Publishing Company, 1955.

60. Koyck, L. M., *Distributed Lags and Investment Analysis,* Amsterdam: North-Holland Publishing Company, 1954.

61. Lerner, A. P., "On the Marginal Product of Capital and the Marginal Efficiency of Investment," *Journal of Political Economy,* 1953, pp. 1–14.

62. Lintner, J., "The Financing of Corporations," *The Corporation in Modern Society,* E. Mason, ed., Cambridge, Mass.: Harvard University Press, 1961, pp. 166–201.

63. Lutz, F. A., and V. C. Lutz, *The Theory of Investment of the Firm,* Princeton, N. J.: Princeton University Press, 1951.

64. Madansky, A., "The Fitting of Straight Lines If Both Variables Are Subject to Error," *Journal of the American Statistical Association,* 1959, pp. 173–205.

65. Makower, H., "Outline of the Problem and Conclusions," Part I from "The Analogy Between Producer and Consumer Equilibrium Analysis," *Economica,* 1950, pp. 63–80.

66. Mansfield, E., "Entry, Gibrat's Law, Innovation, and the Growth of Firms," *American Economic Review,* 1962, pp. 1023–1051.

67. ———, "Technical Change and the Rate of Imitation," *Econometrica*, 1961, pp. 741–766.

68. March, J. G., and H. A. Simon, *Organizations*, Englewood Cliffs, N. J.: Prentice-Hall, Inc., 1958.

69. Meade, J. E., and P. W. S. Andrews, "Summary of Replies to Questions on Effects of Interest Rates," *Oxford Economic Papers*, 1938, pp. 14–31.

70. Meiselman, D., *The Term Structure of Interest Rate*, Englewood Cliffs, N. J.: Prentice-Hall, Inc., 1962.

71. Meltzer, A. H., "The Demand for Money: The Evidence from the Time Series," *Journal of Political Economy*, June 1963, pp. 219–246.

72. ———, and K. Brunner, "The Place of Financial Intermediaries in the Transmission of Monetary Policy," *American Economic Review*, May 1963.

73. Meyer, J. R., and E. Kuh, *The Investment Decision*, Cambridge, Mass.: Harvard University Press, 1957.

74. Minhas, B. S., "The Homohypallagic Production Function, Factor-Intensity Reversals, and The Heckscher-Ohlin Theorem," *Journal of Political Economy*, 1962, pp. 138–162.

75. Modigliani, F., "Comment," *Problems of Capital Formation*, Studies in Income and Wealth, Vol. 19, National Bureau of Economic Research, New York, 1957, pp. 450–463.

76. ———, and R. Brumberg, "Utility Analysis and the Consumption Function," *Post-Keynesian Economics*, K. Kurihara, ed.

77. ———, and M. Miller, "Dividend Policy, Growth and the Valuation of Shares," *Journal of Business*, 1961, pp. 411–433.

78. ———, ———, "Reply," *American Economic Review*, 1959, pp. 655–669.

79. ———, ———, "The Cost of Capital, Corporation Finance and the Theory of Investment," *American Economic Review*, 1958, pp. 261–297.

80. ———, and H. M. Weingartner, "Forecasting Uses of Anticipatory Data on Investment and Sales," *Quarterly Journal of Economics*, 1958, pp. 23–54.

81. ———, and M. Zeman, "The Effect of the Availability of Funds, and the Terms Thereof, on Business Investment," *Conference in Research and Finance,* National Bureau of Economic Research, New York, 1952, pp. 263–309.

82. Moore, G. H., ed., *Business Cycle Indicators,* National Bureau of Economic Research, Princeton, N. J.: Princeton University Press, 1961, 2 vols.

83. Morgan Guaranty Trust Company, *The Morgan Guaranty Survey,* New York, January 1963.

84. Mosak, J. L., *General-Equilibrium Theory in International Trade,* Bloomington, Ind.: Principia Press, Inc., 1944.

85. Muth, J. F., "Rational Expectations and the Theory of Price Movements," *Econometrica,* 1961, pp. 315–335.

86. ———, "Optimal Properties of Exponentially Weighted Forecasts," *Journal of the American Statistical Association,* 1960, pp. 299–306.

87. Muth, R., "The Demand for Non-Farm Housing," in Harberger, *The Demand for Durable Goods,* Chicago: University of Chicago Press, 1960, pp. 29–96.

88. Nerlove, M., "Adaptive Expectations and Cobweb Phenomena," *Quarterly Journal of Economics,* 1958, pp. 227–240.

89. Okun, A. M., "The Predictive Value of Surveys of Business Intentions," *American Economic Review,* May 1962, pp. 218–225.

90. ———, "The Value of Anticipations Data in Forecasting National Product," *Quality and Economic Significance of Anticipations Data,* New York: National Bureau of Economic Research, 1960, pp. 407–451.

91. Patinkin, D., *Money Interest and Prices,* New York: Harper & Row, Publishers, 1956.

92. Pigou, A. C., "Economic Progress in a Stable Environment," *Economica,* 1947.

93. Robinson, J., "The Production Function and the Theory of Capital," *Review of Economic Studies,* 1953–54.

94. Samuelson, P. A., *Foundations of Economic Analysis,* Cambridge, Mass.: Harvard University Press, 1947.

95. Schmookler, J., "Invention, Innovation, and Business Cycles," in *Variability of Private Investment in Plant and Equipment,* Part II, Washington, D.C., 1962.

96. Schumpeter, J. A., *Business Cycles: A Theoretical, Historical and Statistical Analysis of the Capitalist Process* (2 vols.), New York, 1939.

97. ———, "The Explanation of the Business Cycle," *Economica,* 1927.

98. Simon, H. A., "Decision-Making as an Economic Resource," forthcoming.

99. Solow, R. M., "Technological Change and the Aggregate Production Function," *Review of Economics and Statistics,* 1957, pp. 312–320.

100. ———, "A Contribution to the Theory of Economic Growth," *Quarterly Journal of Economics,* 1956, pp. 65–94.

101. ———, "The Production Function and the Theory of Capital," *Review of Economic Studies,* 1955–56, pp. 101–108.

102. Smith, V. L., *Investment and Protection,* Cambridge, Mass.: Harvard University Press, 1961.

103. Tershis, L., "The Elasticity of the Marginal Efficiency Function," *American Economic Review,* 1961, pp. 958–985.

104. Terborgh, G., *60 Years of Business Capital Formation,* Washington, D.C.: Machinery and Allied Products Institute, Council for Technological Advancement, 1960.

105. Theil, H., *Linear Aggregation of Economic Relations,* Amsterdam: North-Holland Publishing Company, 1954.

106. Tinbergen, J., *Statistical Testing of Business Cycle Theories,* Geneva: League of Nations, 1938.

107. Tobin, J., "Money, Capital and Other Stores of Value," *Proceedings of the American Economist Association,* 1961, pp. 26–37.

108. ———, "A Dynamic Aggregative Model," *Journal of Political Economy,* 1955, pp. 103–115.

109. Turvey, R., *Interest Rates and Asset Prices,* London: The Macmillan Company, 1961.

110. United States Government, Department of Commerce, *Business Cycle of Developments.*

111. ———, *Historical Statistics of the United States, Colonial Times to 1957,* 1960.

112. ———, *Survey of Current Business.*

113. ———, *U.S. Income and Output, 1958.*

114. Wellisz, S., "Entrepreneur's Risk, Lender's Risk, and Investment," *Review of Economic Studies,* 1952–53, pp. 105–114.

115. White, W. H., "The Changing Criteria in Investment Planning," *The Variability of Private Investment,* Washington, D.C., Part II, 1962, pp. 1–24.

116. ———, "Interest Inelasticity of Investment Demand—The Case from Business Attitude Surveys Examined," *American Economic Review,* 1956, pp. 565–587.

117. Williamson, D. E., and L. Abbott, "Comments," *American Economic Review,* 1961, pp. 1099–1110.

118. Winfrey, R., *Statistical Analysis of Industrial Property Retirements,* Iowa Engineering Experiment Station, Bulletin 125.